After graduating from Cambridge and the Royal
College of Art, David Wickers has worked
primarily as a freelance writer in various fields,
including TV comedy, children's books, travel
and investigative journalism. He has taught both
in schools and colleges and has travelled widely in
Western and Eastern Europe, North and South
America, West and North Africa and the Middle
East.

THE COMPLETE URBAN FARMER

growing your own
fruit and vegetables
in town

by
David Wickers

with drawings by Sharon Finmark

Fontana/Collins

First published by
Julian Friedmann Publishers Ltd, 1976
First issued in Fontana 1977
Copyright text © David Wickers 1976
Copyright drawings © Sharon Finmark 1976
Book designed by Jacque Solomons
Made and printed in Great Britain by
Fletcher & Son Ltd, Norwich

to Devito, Luigi
and his family in Amaroni

ACKNOWLEDGEMENTS
The author would like to thank the following for
their kind assistance:
Henry Doubleday Research Association
Fisons Ltd., Stewart Plastics Ltd.
Sudbury Technical Products Ltd.
The Editor, *Northern Gardener*
Dept. of Horticulture, Univ. of Illinois
Suttons Seeds Ltd.
The Soil Association
Carters Tested Seeds Ltd.
Humex Ltd.
Metallic Ltd. (Heating Dept.)
Nichols Garden Nursery, Albany, Oregon
W. Atlee Burpee, Riverside, California
House Plant Corner, Oxford, Maryland
U.S. Department of Agriculture, Washington
The National Institute of Agricultural Botany,
Cambridge

CONTENTS

WHY BOTHER?   1
WHERE WHAT AND HOW: A FEW
PRELIMINARIES   3
Space   3
What to grow   4
MAKING A START: TOOLS FOR THE JOB   6
Outdoor farmers need   7
Indoor farmers need   8
PREPARING A SMALL GARDEN   9
Your soil   9
Digging   9
WAYS TO IMPROVE YOUR SOIL   11
Lime   11
Compost   11
Fertilizers   14
CROP ROTATION   15
PLANNING YOUR LAYOUT   18
A suggested plan for a small back-garden   21
Your sowing, planting and
harvesting year planner   22
RAISING VEGETABLES FROM SEED   23
The seeds   23
When to sow your seeds   25
Sowing seeds outdoors   26
Brassicas and seed-beds   28
Raising seeds indoors   29
Transplanting   32
Seed depth and plant distance guide   34
EXTENDING THE GROWING SEASON WITH
GLASS   35
Why?   35
A greenhouse   36
A cold frame   36
Cloches   37
LOOKING AFTER YOUR GARDEN FARM   38
Watering   38
Weeding   39
Mulching   40
Pests and Diseases   41
Some common pests and how to deal with them   43
GROWING FRUIT AND VEGETABLES WHEN
YOU DON'T OWN ANY LAND   46
Allotments   46
Other peoples gardens   46

Window-boxes 47
Balconies, patios and roofs 49
GROWING INDOORS 51
In the office 54
Switched-on sunshine 54
Growing in the dark — mushrooms 55
OTHER DIM SOULS, SPROUTING
VEGETABLES 56
Hydroponics, or growing plants without soil 57
SOME IDEAS FOR INDOOR FRUIT AND
VEGETABLE CONTAINERS 60
Improvised and recycled 60
Home-made 60
Conventional 62
What to grow without a garden 62
Growing your own herbs 65
A guide to herbs 70
How to grow your own yoghurt 71
The general care of indoor fruits
and vegetables 72
Going away on holiday 73
Children and growing things 75
HOW TO GROW INDIVIDUAL VEGETABLES 79
GROWING FRUIT IN TOWN 142
EATING YOUR FRUIT HARVEST 155
SOME GENERAL TIPS ON COOKING
VEGETABLES 156
Soups and broths 158
STORING FRUIT AND VEGETABLES 159
Freezing 159
Drying 160
Making jams 162
Candied fruit 163
Bottling fruit 164
Pickles 165
Chutneys 165
Sauces and juices 167
Salting 167
METRIC CONVERSION CHART 168
FURTHER READING 169
INDEX 173

WHY BOTHER?

Many city people now dream about living off the land, in some gentle rural haven where urban noises, fumes and pressures are far away. But for every one who actually makes the move towards such a self-sufficient life style, hundreds more remain town-tied.

Sadly, only a few urbanites use the resources for growing their own food that are at their disposal. Back-gardens generally sprout just a postage-stamp lawn and a few flowers, only washing lines bloom on high rise balconies, and apartment window-sills are bare. Cellars and attics are an excuse for keeping things which have outlived their useful lives, and, apart from the living-room, which may have a tired bunch of flowers or a couple of potted plants, the rest of the rooms in the house or flat are likely to be untapped growing potential. For the town and city dweller, food grows on the shelves of the local supermarket.

During the Second World War in Britain, as a result of the Dig For Victory campaign, over 10% of the national food production came from gardens and allotments. The Ministry of Agriculture appealed: 'You can help feed yourselves and others . . . The results of your work are of vital national importance.' Today, as people are beginning to realize that a family can basically feed itself from a small area of land, fruit and vegetable growing at home is receiving fresh attention. It is beginning to win back some of those leisure hours lost to competing attractions, such as television. This book will show you just how it can be done, irrespective of whether you are one of the more fortunate townsfolk who do have a small back-garden or yard, or live in a flat, in which case you have a great deal more growing power than you probably imagine. And when you've succeeded in growing your own fruit and vegetables, this book will suggest some good things to do with them.

1

The advantages of home-grown food are enormous. Inflation has, of course, hit the prices of fruit and vegetables just like any other commodity. But shop prices have to pay for the work of the farmers, processors, the packagers, the distributors and the retailers, so that the price of a pound of peas gets pushed up at every stage in the food production chain. In comparison, the price of the original seed packet is minimal — in value for money terms it can represent a return of more than 1,000% on your seed investment if you bother to raise your own.

Seeds can almost grow on their own, but they really appreciate some effort and care on your behalf to bring them to fruition. You need spend no more time as an urban farmer than half the time you spend shopping, and you will certainly avoid some of those lunch-time struggles, Friday night queues, parking difficulties and heavy loads. Your main food store can be just a few steps away from the kitchen. The problem of last-minute arrivals for the evening meal can be solved with a few strides into the garden or on to the balcony.

Home-grown and harvested vegetables are fresher than any you can find in the shops. They are, after all, only minutes away from the dinner table, rather than days or weeks. This not only delights your taste buds, but also means that your diet will be more nutritious since many vegetables rapidly begin to lose their vitamin content after they have been gathered. Yours are going to be less contaminated, too, than the artificially fertilized, insecticided, colourized and flavourized fruit and vegetables of the big-scale commercial producers. But, to get the most from your fruit and vegetables, they should either be enjoyed in the raw state, or prepared and cooked appropriately, and never overcooked. In terms of both health and flavour, home-grown vegetables will then rival the costliest cuts of meat.

The not-so-fresh vegetables that you do find

in the shops are those that are in general demand and so justify large-scale production and distribution. The shopkeeper can only cater for majority tastes, and so the choices are limited, unless you live in an affluent suburb and are prepared to pay for a wide variety. For the same reasons, small and tender varieties of vegetables are simply uneconomical. For example, tomatoes are bred with tough skins to enable them to travel well. Grow your own vegetables and you can enjoy exactly what you like from artichokes to zuccini, and at times of the year when the more familiar vegetables have not yet appeared in the shops.

The skills of growing fruit and vegetables at home are not hard to acquire. You do not need a fanatical interest and devotion. You choose what you want — the quick and easy varieties if you like — start them off properly and help them on their way. The odd bouts of physical exercise that are involved will probably be lacking in your normal daily town routine anyway.

You can derive both economies and endless pleasure from providing your own food in the most unfarmlike of circumstances, and in your spare time. Your home-grown fruits and vegetables will not only be delicious to eat, but really spectacular to look at, beautiful enough to stand where only flowers are considered normal. Every house or flat has room for a green revolution.

WHERE, WHAT AND HOW: A FEW PRELIMINARIES
Space

The first problem that the urban farmer is likely to face is limited space. But before you start to worry, just take stock of your growing resources — they will be more than you think.

Measure the size of your garden or back yard if you have one. Draw a scale plan on graph paper at this stage (it will be useful later on for planning the fruit and vegetable layout). If the space seems no bigger than a pocket handkerchief, measure it all the same. Every inch has a growing potential.

Do you have a balcony? How big is it? Will it safely support the weight of tubs, pots and boxes full of earth?

Are there any patios, sun-lounges, glass-sided home extensions, conservatories or other bright and sunny areas?

How many window-sills can you get at?

Are there any cellar or basement areas that can be used? Or attics and lofts? Cupboards under the stairs? Is there access to the roof and a flat area that would support tubs and the like (remember that earth is very heavy)?

Don't neglect your city offices. They have window-sills too, and probably lots of other spaces for you to grow contributions to your mid-week lunches.

What to grow

GOOD YIELDERS
broad beans
dwarf french beans
runner beans
beetroot
carrots
lettuce
courgette/marrow
onions
tomatoes
swiss chard

EASY TO GROW
broad beans
dwarf french beans
runner beans
beetroot
carrots
swiss chard
spinach
parsnips
turnips
lettuce
radishes
onions
kale

Obviously, just what you like to eat. But it may not be quite as simple as that.

In the first place there is the problem of space. Unless you have a large — 40' by 30'- ish garden — you will not be able to become entirely self-sufficient in vegetables. But there again you may not want to be. You should avoid growing vegetables that take up a lot of your precious room or occupy the ground for a long time, unless you are really crazy about them. Maincrop potatoes (not the small and delicious earlies), parsnips, Brussels sprouts, cabbages and big fruit trees are all really a bit too grand in scale for small town-growers. Also, by the time these have reached maturity on your 'farm' they are also in abundance in the shops and fairly cheap to buy.

Go for vegetables that taste better when home grown and eaten fresh. These include peas, radishes, lettuces, beans, cauliflowers, asparagus, tomatoes and sweet corn, which all tend to

4

lose their value soon after picking. This 'soil to supper' interval is not nearly so important with maincrop potatoes, celery, parsnips and other root crops, for example.

Be adventurous in your choices, especially if the fruits and vegetables that you like are generally not available in the shops, or only at an exorbitant price. Many of the commonplace vegetables have similar, but relatively uncommon, substitutes that are often superior in taste. Grow salsify, a sort of oystery-tasting vegetable, instead of the boring old turnip. As long as the substitutes yield as much actual vegetable per space as what they are substitutes for, and are not any harder to grow, they should always be chosen in preference. Only trial and error will tell you that, so don't be afraid to experiment.

You cannot grow any type of fruit and vegetable everywhere. Not only will space limit your choices, but so will your climate. You can't grow melons outdoors in Alaska, and your summer lettuces will be sure to suffer if you live where the midday sun is hot. But, by compensating for your climate — for instance, growing under glass in a dull climate — and by selecting the right varieties of fruit and vegetables for your area, you will be able to overcome some of these limitations. It is impossible to lay down any hard and fast rules about this. A sound way to begin your farming career is to ask other local growers just what flourishes well in your area, with regard to both the yield and the flavour. But do allow for their likely conservatism; local growers do tend to stick to the same old things.

Send off immediately for one or two seed catalogues from seed manufacturers; you will see their advertisements in the Sunday papers and gardening magazines. Catalogues are generally sent free of charge and are a mine of information. Each fruit and vegetable has been developed over the years into a number of different varieties. Some, the 'hardies', are suitable for cool, rainy climates and conditions; some for the opposite, and a lot of other possibilities exist

DON'T MIND THE COLD
cabbage
broad beans
beetroot
carrots
lettuce
onions
Jerusalem artichokes
sprouts
chicory
celery
celeriac
kale
kohl rabi
peas
potatoes
spinach
leeks
radishes
parsnips
salsify (& scorzonera)
turnip
broccoli
asparagus
fennel

GROWING INDOORS
herbs
tomatoes
mushrooms
strawberries
courgettes
cucumbers
lettuce
radishes
alfalfa
mung beans
mustard and cress
salsify or scorzonera

NICE LOOKERS
globe artichokes
asparagus
aubergine
runner beans
peppers
carrots
courgette/marrow
spinach
sweet corn
tomatoes

in between.

As well as talking to experienced local growers about the probability of growing a giant banana tree in your Bronx or Surbiton back yard, you can get advice from other sources, such as local horticultural or allotment societies, nurserymen and gardening centres, U.S. County Agents, State Extension Services, experimental stations, soil conservationists, organic farming societies, and so on. Use your yellow pages or local library to find where these people are.

Any choices you make about things to grow must come down to the needs and wants of you and your family. Why not start off with your ideal cornucopia and work back to reality as you read on? But don't overlook one other vital element in your choices — what the fruits and vegetables look like. In your functional quest for urban survival don't neglect the decorative aspects of your food, especially if you are going to grow it indoors, or in the place of decorative flowers and shrubbery. The table on page 5 will help you, but you can start out with the confidence that most of the things you will grow will look prettier than you might think, especially since you normally see the products without their often delightful foliage. When you replace the classic bowl of fruit as the coffee table centrepiece with an arrangement of tomatoes, aubergines and peppers you will really have reached the height of fruit and vegetable aesthetics.

MAKING A START: TOOLS FOR THE JOB

There is a vast range of makes and types of gardening tools on the market and as many places to buy them.

Don't get obsessed with gadgets, as most are a waste of money. But do buy the best quality tools that you can afford, and always a well-known make. Cheap tools are false economy — they will not last long.

Outdoor farmers need

(in rough order of importance):

SPADE
For winter digging. Make sure that the handle and length feel comfortable to use.

FORK
For digging and breaking down lumpy soils. And for lifting root crops. Look for the same qualities as in a spade.

DUTCH HOE
For weeding and breaking up the surface of the soil during the growing season.

HAND TROWEL AND FORK
For planting, weeding and thinning.

GARDEN LINE
For marking out straight rows. Make your own from two stakes and garden twine.

RAKE
For making the soil fine and crumbly for sowing. The edge can also be used for making shallow drills.

MEASURING ROD
A 10' length of wood, marked every 3", to measure rows and distances between plants.

WATERING-CAN
Buy a big two-gallon one (to save on journeys to and from the tap) with two 'roses', a fine one for seedlings and a coarser one for general use. Buy a second, smaller can for liquid fertilizers or insecticides.

HOSE
For anything other than the smallest of gardens. Better to use one without a sprinkler.

DRAW HOE
Not absolutely essential but useful for making seed 'drills', or rows, and earthing-up jobs (see 'potatoes').

DIBBER
For making holes for seedlings (make one from a broken spade or fork handle).

NETS
To protect seeds and seedlings from birds — make your own from cotton and sticks, or use nylon netting.

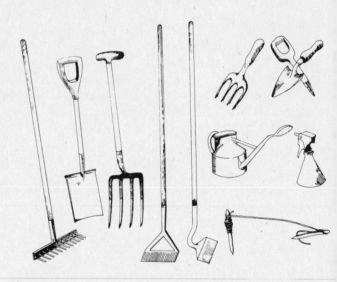

Indoor farmers need

Indoor farmers need a lot less: a hand trowel and fork, a dibber, a watering-can (all smaller than those for outdoor use) and a fine water sprayer for watering leaves.

Your tools will have long and healthy lives if you look after them. Wipe off the earth after use, wash and rub them with some rough material and wipe with an oily rag before putting them away.

The major cost of urban farming will be tool-buying, but the total will be less than the cheapest TV set or a modest camera. After the initial investment, your annual seed, fertilizer and odds-and-ends bill will be less than half that amount.

PREPARING A SMALL GARDEN
Your soil

You will be very lucky if your soil is perfect, one that combines sand, clay, chalk and humus in the right proportions. The best type of soil to have is called a 'loam'; it never gets too dry or waterlogged, is fertile and easy to cultivate.

Your soil may well be too clayey, sticking to your boots and tools, heavy to work and often getting waterlogged during times of heavy rain. Or it may be too sandy, gritty to touch, and always in need of watering. Plants often die of thirst or hunger, since vital nutrients are carried away by the rain.

All types of soil have their pros and cons. You obviously can't change yours, but you can compensate for its deficiencies and be able to grow most fruits and vegetables without any great problems. The more time you devote to preparing your soil the better the final results will be. The major reason for poor vegetables is a poor soil.

Digging

First of all dig it, as soon in the autumn as possible, but not when the ground is frozen or wet. Digging breaks down the soil and lets the air, rain, wind and frost get at it to break it down even further. Here's how to dig a garden properly, with minimum backache:

— stretch a line between two sticks at one end of the garden. This will help you to dig in straight lines.
— spread some peat over the land to be dug, as this will improve its general texture and make it easier to dig and, later, to hoe and rake. (Peat will also help to improve the drainage of clay soils and the water-retaining capabilities of sandy soils.)

— take your spade and start to dig. Make a trench about 4" wide and to the depth of the spade blade (known as a 'spit') right across the end where you put the line. Keep the spade vertical and cut the soil in cubes. Pile up the soil at the other end of the garden (the bigger your patch, the more useful a wheelbarrow would be).

— add compost along the bottom of the open trench (see later).

— dig a second trench, just behind the first, turning the cubes of soil over and into the open trench (on top of the compost). Carry on in this way until you reach the end.

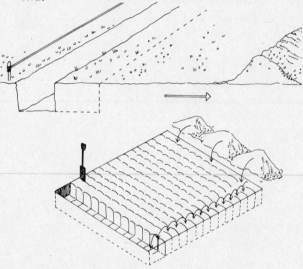

If you start to hit big stones or a layer of chalk below the surface keep your digging a bit shallower. Annual weeds, those without thick roots, can be buried in as your dig, but you must remove the perennial roots (like docks, thistles and nettles) as you go, or else they will constantly plague you. Burn them.

Take your digging easy. Watch an old-timer doing it, lighting up his pipe between rows, and deriving real pleasure from the activity. Now for the nasty news. If you have really clayey soil that becomes bog-like after a shower of rain, you should dig it to a double spit depth and put sand and builder's rubble in the lower trench to improve the drainage.

Gardens only need one thorough annual dig, but in the spring you should dig or fork over again and break down any of the big lumps of soil that have not been fragmented by the weather.

WAYS TO IMPROVE YOUR SOIL
Lime

Clay soils benefit from the addition of lime. It makes them easier to work, stimulates important bacterial activity, releases plant food that is already present in the soil and adds calcium. It also corrects 'acidity'.

Most legumes (the pea and bean family) prefer a slightly acid soil, but in general you should try and get a good balance between acidity and alkalinity. Test your soil before throwing lime on indiscriminately, either with a strip of soil-testing paper or tape, or, more accurately, by using a soil-testing kit. These are simple to use — you mix up some samples of soil with the test chemicals and identify certain colour changes with the help of a chart. Some borough, county horticultural depts, U.S. agricultural county agents etc. may be able to tell you about the nature of your neighbourhood soil. If you find that your soil is too acid, then spread lime on the surface and let it weather in, sometime in the winter. If too alkaline, add fallen leaves or bonemeal.

Compost

The person with a small garden should do everything possible to get the most out of the area at his disposal.

Plants need certain things in order to grow. They breathe and drink, and so need carbon, oxygen and hydrogen which they obtain from

air and water. They also need:
— nitrogen for their general growth and the development of their leaves;
— phosphorous for their roots and the ripening of seeds and fruit;
— potash for the general health of the plants and resistance to pests and diseases;

All growing plants use up these foods from the soil, and it is vital to put them back in again. The more you want to use your soil, the more important this becomes. One of the best ways to do this is to put back as much organic matter as possible.

Humus is the name given to animal and vegetable matter in the soil which has been broken down into plant food by fungi and bacteria. It is therefore 'organic'; soil without humus is just finely ground rock.

The most obvious form of organic waste matter that you can put into your soil is animal manure, after it has been left to rot and ferment naturally. Some years ago the town dweller could have followed the horses in the street with a bucket and spade, but today, unless you live near a riding stable, you won't find animal manure. You can buy bagged, and unsmelly, manure (such as hop manure).

The small town-gardener can easily make his own organic compost out of natural waste material, thereby re-cycling it in the most useful way imaginable. The Chinese have been at it for 4,000 years. You can either buy a ready-made composting unit, designed for a small garden, or make one. Bash four posts into the ground to make a three-foot square, and surround it on three sides with wire netting or wooden boards. Or remove the top and bottom from an oil drum or dustbin, drill holes in the sides and stand it on a layer of bricks — a tidier arrangement.

What can be put on your town compost? Basically: if it grows, it can be composted, except for disease- or pest-ridden material, perennial weeds (the ones with roots) or weeds that have gone to seed, fat or grease, holly, ivy or any garden rubbish larger than a twig. The following are all welcome: household food scraps (eggshells, fruit and vegetable peelings, coffee grounds, leftover food, etc.) sawdust, paper, lawn cuttings (also from neighbours and parks provided it has not been sprayed with poisonous weed-killer), leafmould, hair cuttings, smaller hedge clippings, dead flowers, prunings, weeds, wood ashes, sea-weeds, and so on.

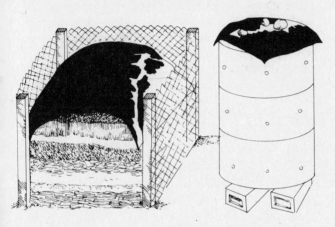

Variety is the spice of your compost heap. You can buy proprietary brands of activators to speed up the rotting process.

A compost must be built up in layers:

9" layer of vegetable waste
activator
9" layer of vegetable waste
an activator — nitro-chalk to help the rotting process in place of manure
cinders (or use straw or broken twigs) to allow the air to circulate
a soil base — fairly well dug

Keep the pile moist (even pee on it occasionally) and add an odd sprinkling of lime to counteract the acidity brought about by the rotting process. Protect the compost with black polythene sheeting, to keep the rain off and retain the heat. Poke holes in the side to let the air get in. Turn the compost with a fork, sides to middle, once a month.

The compost has to be well rotted before being dug into the soil (or used as a mulch — see later). In the summer the process will take around three months, in the winter about six. When it is ready it will look like brown sludge and the original ingredients should not be discernible.

Composting is an ideal way of returning foods to the soil. It also improves its texture and drainage, making clay soils easier to work and sandy soils more retentive of water. Soils that have been composted warm up earlier in the spring and stay cooler during the summer.

Fertilizers

The addition of fertilizers won't actually improve the structure of your soil but it will help your fruits and vegetables to grow. Fertilizer should never be regarded as a substitute for organic compost, just as a supplement, a tomato tonic or pea pick-me-up.

Use a general or balanced fertilizer that contains nitrogen, phosphorous and potassium. Rake it into the top few inches of soil about ten days before sowing or planting (and never at the same time as lime) and water it in well. Read the instructions on the packet carefully and *never* overdo it. You should also sprinkle some round the plants (or 'top dress') during the growing season. A liquid fertilizer will be the most convenient type to use indoors but be careful not to let it fall on the plant itself. Steer clear of inorganic fertilizers, those that are made from minerals or factory processes (as well as inorganic pest and disease control — see

later). There are several organic or natural
fertilizers on the market that are made up from
the waste products of food industries, such as
bonemeal and dried blood. They will do you,
and your soil, more good.

Both composting and the addition of
fertilizer and lime depend on what you plan to
grow and where you plan to put it. Some crops
prefer a well manured and composted soil, for
example, while others do much better in soil
that has been manured for a previous crop. You
must first plan out your crop rotation.

CROP ROTATION

The idea of crop rotation probably sounds more
applicable to a thousand-acre farm than a small
back-garden. But it shouldn't be.

With the exception of your permanent crops
that stay in the same place from year to year
(such as asparagus, rhubarb and globe artichokes)
no single crop should be grown on the same
piece of land for two years running. Why not?
 – different vegetables take different nutrients
    or foods from the soil – cabbage takes a lot
    of nitrogen, for instance, beans help to put
    it back – and so single-crop farming,
    without rotation, on any scale, means that
    very heavy fertilization is necessary to put
    back the goodness in the soil.
 – rotation also prevents the build-up of pests
    and diseases that take a fancy to a particular
    vegetable (club root attacks the cabbage
    family, for example, so moving the
    cabbages around helps to prevent the
    disease).
In the most minuscule of gardens, where rotation
is out of the question, you should at least make
sure that you change the vegetable rows or
sitings around each year. But rotate if you can,
as follows:
Vegetables can be divided into three broad
groups, according to what they take from the

soil and their vulnerability to certain pests and diseases.

LEGUMES

(peas and beans). Celery, chicory, onion, leeks, tomatoes and sweet corn also fit into this category.

BRASSICAS

(greens) — cabbage, Brussels sprouts, spinach, kohl-rabi, kale, broccoli, cauliflower, etc.

ROOTS

potatoes, carrots, parsnips, Jerusalem artichokes, celeriac, salisfy, scorzonera, beetroot, etc.

Since different crops have different needs it follows that you should fertilize/compost/ manure/lime according to the vegetable group that will occupy the area of land each year.

LEGUMES

like well manured or composted ground.

BRASSICAS

need lime to prevent club root disease plus a general fertilizer.

ROOTS

just need a light general fertilizer before sowing; and always grow them on land manured for a previous crop — in other words they should follow the legumes (only potatoes like recently manured ground but not lime).

Divide your garden into three equal sections and plan to change your layout round each year as the diagram shows. If your garden is too small to bother with root crops you could just work a two-year rotation between the brassicas and a mixture of the others.

1st Year	2nd Year	3rd Year	4th Year
A LEGUMES Manure	C ROOTS GF	B BRASSICAS Lime/GF	A LEGUMES Manure
B BRASSICAS Lime/GF	A LEGUMES Manure	C ROOTS GF	B BRASSICAS Lime/GF
C ROOTS GF	B BRASSICAS Lime/GF	A LEGUMES Manure	C ROOTS GF

GF = General Fertilizer

The arrangement of your crop rotation should be the first step in planning the layout of your garden. Here are some other general positional factors to think about:
— all vegetables and fruits like to grow in sunny, well-drained and sheltered positions; leafy vegetables can stand more shade than root vegetables, which in turn can stand more shade than vegetable fruit plants (cucumbers, peppers, tomatoes, etc.)
— your rows should run from north to south to prevent shading, (or from east to west if your garden slopes from north to south)
— allow space, if you can afford it, along one side for any permanent beds (perennials, like asparagus, that do not need to be replanted each year), your compost, a small seed-bed, a cold frame or a greenhouse. To fit all of these into a city garden will probably be impossible but after reading this book you will be able to decide which are most important to you.

PLANNING YOUR LAYOUT

To avoid wasting time, seeds, money, land and lots of effort, it is crucial for a limited-space gardener to plan everything on paper. By using the charts, sowing-tables, depth and distance information in this book, as well as the seed catalogues, you will be able to draw up a scaled plan of what your garden will look like and see just what will fit in. On page 21 there is also a suggested small-garden plan that you may prefer to use, making substitutes here and there to suit your own tastes.

Apart from the basic knowledge of how to grow fruits and vegetables, there are several techniques, which are easy to learn, that enable the urban farmer get the most out of the growing spaces available:

You must choose from the seed catalogue the most suitable variety of fruit or vegetable for your particular climate. But varieties also differ according to the size of the plant they produce. Both indoor and outdoor town gardeners will gain valuable space by picking the small — 'dwarf', 'mini', 'babyheaded', 'stump-rooted' and 'bush' — varieties. A line of fruit 'cordons' — single stems which are trained to grow against a wall or fence — could take up no more space than a row of Brussels sprouts. And a small variety does not necessarily imply a smaller yield.

There are also 'early', 'main' and 'late' varieties. By juggling around with different combinations you will be able to grow more than one crop in the same ground in the same year. The early varieties are so called because they produce a crop in the shortest time and can be harvested, and the ground cleared in time for a following main crop. These techniques are known as 'catch' cropping (or succession cropping if you are describing the planting of a late variety after the land has been cleared of an earlier main crop). In effect you can double, or even triple, the size of your land.

Many vegetables are quick-maturing or have quick-maturing varieties. They can be planted in the same ground at the same time as slower maturing vegetables that will be occupying the ground for most of the growing season. Swiss chard, spinach, lettuces and radishes for example can be planted with salsify, parsnips and Brussels sprouts. The quick maturers are ready to be harvested before the slower ones are ready to occupy the whole space. The quick maturers can also be planted between slower growing vegetables before the latter need the room for expansion. This is known as 'intercropping' (which also refers to planting between tall crops that need quite a distance in between them to prevent their shading each other; root crops like turnips can be planted between rows of peas, beans and corn for example). But remember tall plants should be planted on the north side, so that they don't cast a shadow over everything else.

Stagger the sowing of vegetables throughout the season wherever possible, to give you a continuous supply of fresh vegetables, rather than a glut at one particular time and shortages for the rest of the year. This is known as 'successional' sowing (not to be confused with 'succession cropping', just mentioned). You can plan to re-sow every two weeks, or when the last batch of seeds appears as seedlings. Storing your vegetables (see page 159) is also an important part of small-space gardening as this helps both to avoid wastes and winter shortages. You should also sow vegetables for 'overwintering', giving you crops early in the spring, before they are seen in the shops.

Garden vertically by using all the fences and walls you can for growing climbing and trailing varieties of fruits and vegetables (like trailing marrows, cucumbers, beans, peas, tomatoes; fruits, especially, are adaptable to being trained up against a flat surface, provided it faces the sun). If you don't have any fences, make your own trellis supports, or wigwam tripods for climbers.

Extend your growing season, and therefore really the size of your garden, by using glass (cloches, cold frames and greenhouses — see page 35). You will be able to sow your crops earlier in spring and later into autumn, and also grow exciting things that are not possible outdoors in a cool climate, like peppers, aubergines and melons.

If you live in a town and have a garden don't be smug about the section on growing indoors. Use all the resources at your disposal, and grow things indoors as well as in the open. When planning your garden layout don't include those fruits and vegetables that can be grown perfectly satisfactorily, and often better, indoors. Also, by raising your plants from seeds indoors the precious ground will be occupied for less time, leaving room for other things like 'catch crops'.

Although you'll want to grow the most you can from your various fruit and vegetable patches, don't cram plants together at less than the recommended planting distances. You must give them the space and light they need. The charts have been worked out to the minimum spacing already and any further economizing will mean poor specimens. But be prepared for some failures, and learn by your own experiences. Keep a record of your planting dates, the yield of a particular plant (whether you grew too much or too little in relation to your needs), the variety, the weather, when you harvested and the general performance of your fruits and vegetables. Such a record will be of great help

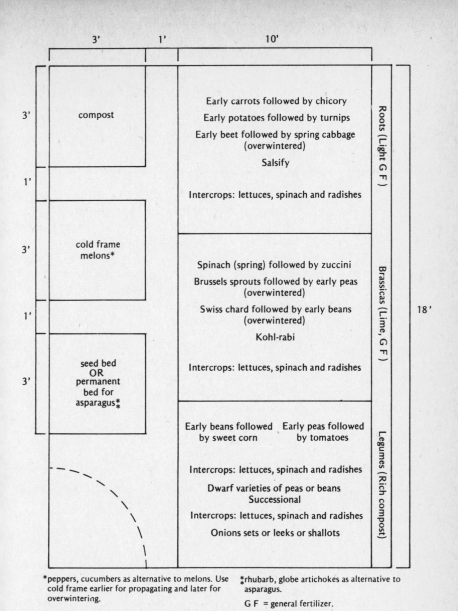

	3'	1'	10'	

compost

cold frame melons*

seed bed OR permanent bed for asparagus**

Early carrots followed by chicory

Early potatoes followed by turnips

Early beet followed by spring cabbage (overwintered)

Salsify

Intercrops: lettuces, spinach and radishes

Spinach (spring) followed by zuccini

Brussels sprouts followed by early peas (overwintered)

Swiss chard followed by early beans (overwintered)

Kohl-rabi

Intercrops: lettuces, spinach and radishes

Early beans followed by sweet corn   Early peas followed by tomatoes

Intercrops: lettuces, spinach and radishes

Dwarf varieties of peas or beans Successional

Intercrops: lettuces, spinach and radishes

Onions sets or leeks or shallots

Roots (Light G F)

Brassicas (Lime, G F)

Legumes (Rich compost)

3' 1' 3' 1' 3'   18'

*peppers, cucumbers as alternative to melons. Use cold frame earlier for propagating and later for overwintering.

**rhubarb, globe artichokes as alternative to asparagus.

G F = general fertilizer.

when you start to make next year's plans.

A suggested plan for a small 18' by 10' back-garden, showing how any extra space can house a cold frame, compost heap and perennial bed or seed-bed. It should be combined with the indoor cultivation of mushrooms, sprouting vegetables, peppers, aubergines, herbs, strawberries, cucumber, plus propagation of seeds.

YOUR SOWING, PLANTING AND HARVESTING YEAR PLANNER

The dates given here apply to a British climate, but growing times for other areas will be similar.

year 1 = JAN–DEC, year 2 = JAN–JUN. Where a cell shows two values "X/Y", the upper value (harvest, etc.) is over the lower (sowing, etc.).

	JAN	FEB	MAR	APR	MAY	JUN	JUL	AUG	SEP	OCT	NOV	DEC	JAN	FEB	MAR	APR	MAY	JUN
Artichokes, Globe				PPP														HH
Artichokes, Jerusalem		XX	XXX	XXX					H	HHH	HHH	H						
Asparagus			PP	PPP	P													HH
Aubergine			G	GGG	GXX	XXX		HHH	HHH									
Bean, Broad		GGG	GGX	XXX		HH	HHH	HHH	H	WWW	WW							
Bean, Dwarf French			GG	GXX	XXX	XXH	HHH	HHH	HHH	HHH								
Bean, Runner				GGG	GGX	XXX	XHH	HHH	HHH	HHH								
Beetroot				XXX	XXX	XXX	H/XHH	HHH	HHH	HHH		/						
Broccoli (sprouting)			GGS	SSS	SSP	PPP	PP		HH	HHH	HHH	HHH	HHH					
Brussels Sprouts	G	GGG	GGS	SSS	PPP	PPP			HH	HHH	HHH	HHH	HHH	HH				
Cabbage, Spring						SSS	SSS	PPP	PPP							HH	HHH	HHH
Cabbage, Summer	G	GGG	GGS	SSS	SPP	PPP	HHH/P	HHH	HHH	HHH								
Cabbage, Winter Savoy				SSS	PP/SSS	PPP	P		HH	HHH	HHH	HHH	HHH	HHH	H			
Carrots		GGG	GGX	XXX	HH/XXX	HHH/XXX	HHH/X	HHH	HHH	HHH								
Cauliflower		GGG	GGS	SSS	PPP/SSS	PPP/S	H	HHH	HHH	HHH	HHH	H						
Celery (and Celeriac)			GGG	GGX	XXX	XX		HHH	HHH	HHH								
Chard, Swiss				PPP	PPP	PPP	HH/PP	HHH	HHH	HHH	H							
Chicory				X	XXX	X			HHH	HHH	HHH	HHH	HHH	HHH				
Cucumber				GGG	GGX	XXX		HHH	HHH	H								
Fennel				XX	XXX	XXX	HHH/XXX	HHH/X	HHH	HHH								
Kale			SSS			PPP		H	HHH									
Kohl-rabi				XXX	XXX	XXX	HHH/XXX	HHH/XX	HHH	HHH	H							
Leeks		GGG	SSS	SSS		PP	P		HH	HHH	HHH	HHH	HHH	HHH				
Lettuce (and endive)	G	GGG	XXX	H/XXX	HHH/XXX	HHH/XXX	HHH/XXX	HHH/XXX	HHH/XXX	H/WW	W					H	HHH	H
Marrow			G	GGG	XX	XX	HH	HHH	HHH	HHH								
Onion (sets and shallots)		P	PPP	PPP			H	HHH	HHH	HHH								
Parsnip			XXX	XXX	X				H	HHH	HHH	HHH	HHH	HHH	H			
Peas		GGG	XXX	XXX	HH/XXX	HHH/XXX	HHH/X	HHH	HHH	H	W	WWW				HH	H	
Peppers				G	GGG	XX	X	HHH	HHH									
Potatoes (earlies)			GG	GXX	XXX		HHH	HHH	HHH	HHH								
Radishes	G	GGG	GXX	H/XXX	HHH/XXX	HHH/XXX	HHH/XXX	HHH/XXX	HHH/XXX	HHH/XWW	HHH	H						
Salsify (and Scorzonera)				XXX	XXX				HHH	HHH	HHH	HHH	HHH	HHH				
Spinach, Summer		GGG	XXX	XXX	HHH/XXX	HHH/XXX	HHH/X	HHH	HHH	HHH								
Spinach, Winter							XXX	XWW		HHH	HHH	HHH	HHH	HHH	HHH			
Swede				XX	XXX				H	HHH	HHH	HHH	HHH	HHH	H			
Sweet Corn				GG	G	XXX		HHH	HHH	HHH	H							
Tomatoes		G	GGG	GGG		XXX		HHH	HH									
Turnip	GGG	GGG	XX	XXX	XXX	H/XXX	HHH/XXX	HHH/XXX	HHH/XXX	X	HHH	HHH	HH					
	JAN	FEB	MAR	APR	MAY	JUN	JUL	AUG	SEP	OCT	NOV	DEC	JAN	FEB	MAR	APR	MAY	JUN

RAISING VEGETABLES FROM SEED
The seeds

By the beginning of the planting year you should have decided what you are going to grow and be ready to order your seeds from the companies who sent you their catalogues, or from chain stores, hardware shops, gardening centres, and so on. Many of the vegetables that you decide to grow can be bought as ready-raised plants but they are more expensive, not always as good, and certainly less of a personal achievement than raising from seed. Restrict your plant buying to fruits, and those vegetables that are best raised in a heated greenhouse. You can nowadays also buy ready-sown packages of salad or herb collections in their own plastic propagators.

A seed contains an embryo plant with reserves of food to sustain it during its first few hours of life. In the seed catalogues, apart from the varieties listed under each vegetable, you will see references to two other types of seed:

— 'pelleted' seeds are bigger and easier to handle than ordinary seeds, and will save you time, and wastage, later on when it comes to thinning the seedlings, as they can be planted just where you want them to grow (all this will be explained later). Suffice it to say, at this stage, that although they are more expensive than ordinary seeds it is a good idea to buy pelleted carrot and lettuce seeds

23

at least because these are very small and hard to sow, especially if there is a wind blowing.

— *F.1. Hybrids* are raised by controlled fertilization between two selected parents. They are again more expensive but generally produce a heavier and better crop.

If your aim is urban self-sufficiency you can save your own seeds for sowing the following year from your own home produce (except those grown from F.1. Hybrid seeds). With fleshier types of vegetables, cut them open and scoop out the seeds. Wash them and rub them on a sieve to remove all the flesh. Then spread them on paper to dry. Many vegetables will 'go to seed' if they are left in the ground after they have ripened. Leave podded seeds, like peas and beans, on the stem until they dry out on their own accord. Store all seeds in airtight cans, in a cool, dry place. Root vegetables for replanting should be stored throughout the winter and replanted in the spring.

But saving your own seeds rather than buying afresh, is a less reliable way of getting good results, as no controlled pollination will take place and the seeds may become rather poor vegetables. Seed production is a highly skilled job and, for the sake of a few pence per packet, probably best left to the professional seedsmen. Their seeds are also better protected against pests and diseases.

Order your seeds early. In general you will not need more than one packet of each type of vegetable that you want to grow. This may be too much for a small row, so try to join forces with a neighbour and share your packets. You will also find it cheaper to buy seeds through an allotment or horticultural society if you become a member. Well worth doing for the sake of a bit of brain-picking too. If you do find that you are left with seeds at the end of the growing season, store the leftovers in lidded tins in a cool, dry place and they should be all right for the following year, although the success rate of germination will have dropped by a few per cent.

HARDY:
Can withstand frost (but not all of them can
survive in winter outdoors, say in the North-
East USA or Scotland). Sow outdoors in early
spring.

HALF-HARDY:
Need protection against winter frost, but may
be OK in a sheltered patio or against a south-
facing wall. Best off raised under glass and
planted out in the spring.

TENDER:
Must always be raised under glass or indoors
except during a warm summer.

With the exception of a few *perennials* (such as
asparagus, globe artichokes and rhubarb that are
grown as permanent crops and will produce
over a number of years) most vegetables are
grown as annuals, raised from seed and planted
or sown outdoors in late spring. They die in
winter and are renewed annually.

When to sow your seeds

The right time for sowing your seeds, or planting
out seedlings, will depend on where you live as
well as the particular fruit or vegetable that you
want to grow.
   Clearly, if you happen to live in the southern
hemisphere 'spring' will occur when countries in
the northern half of the globe are experiencing
autumn, and vice versa. But even within, say,
the northern hemisphere there are so many
variations in climatic conditions that hard and
fast rules about when to sow, plant and harvest
are meaningless. In the United States, for
example, there are over thirty broad climatic
regions each of which affect the growing of fruit
and vegetables in differing ways. Within Britain
'average' planting schedules may be brought
forward by as much as a month in the south
during a mild spell, or retarded by a month in
the north during harsh weather.

Even relatively small areas may experience a wide variety of conditions, all of which make nonsense of rigid schedules. So many variables play an important part in the growing process, such as the type of soil, latitude, altitude, light, shelter, humidity, temperature (city temperatures are usually 5°−10° F higher than in suburbs), length of day, rainfall, snow, frost (you should know the frost-free date in spring and the first severe frost in autumn for your locality), wind, and, for city growers, pollution. These factors will influence not only what you can grow, but how to grow it, when to grow it, and when you can finally get your teeth into it.

The sowing, planting and harvesting information contained in the section of individual vegetables is meant to serve as a guideline. The year planner on page 22 is also intended as a rough and ready guide as to just what you should be doing when, but it is based on 'average' British conditions. Try and get as much local advice as you can, and above all use your common sense about the weather and the state of your soil. If it is too cold and frosty your seeds will be doomed no matter what the charts and seed packets tell you.

Sowing seeds outdoors

Root crops, hardies and some half-hardy vegetables are usually sown outdoors directly into the ground, which must be well prepared beforehand. After digging, any remaining lumpy bits should be broken down with the back of the fork and any large stones removed, as well as fresh weeds that have appeared since winter digging. Tread over the soil to make it firm and then rake it to a fine, level, crumbly surface, known to the old pros as a fine 'tilth'. If the soil doesn't want to be 'tilthed' some damp peat will help. Try to mould the soil into a ball and then crumble it again − if it forms a ball and crumbles easily, then you'll know its just right for sowing. Water the soil thoroughly before sowing.

If you are adding fertilizer, or 'top dressing' with compost, water and rake it into the top inch or so of soil at least ten days beforehand.

Vegetable seeds are best grown in straight rows. This makes weeding easy because you know just where the plants should be. Use a garden line to make the rows straight and draw the 'draw-hoe' along the line to make a V-shaped trench, or use a ½" bamboo stick or broom handle. The actual depth of the drill will depend on the size of the seeds you are sowing (look at the planting chart on page 34), roughly twice their diameter. The largest seeds can be planted in holes made with a pencil or dibber. Water drills before you sow. Peas and beans are best sown in flat-bottomed drills, about 6" wide and 2" or 3" deep, in a double row.

Not all the seeds in your packet will 'germinate', or grow into seedlings, and eventually full-size vegetables, so you have to cover yourself. You can either sow the seeds fairly close together, and later 'thin' them to their correct planting distances after their leaves have sprouted, or you can plant two or three seeds at each correct planting station (the optimum distance apart for their future development) and later thin them to one plant per hole. The latter method is better for the larger seeds, and the

former for smaller ones. Pelleted seeds are always spaced at their correct growing distance.

To judge the distances along the row use your home-made measuring rod, or a cloth tape. Some seed companies sell seeds already correctly spaced in tapes.

To thin seedlings, place two fingers on the soil on either side of the seedling that is to remain, so that it is not disturbed when its neighbours are lifted. Thinnings can sometimes be eaten (carrots, onions, lettuces and other very tasty youngsters) or transplanted elsewhere (see later) or, more usually, thrown on to the compost heap. You should always thin seedlings as soon as they are big enough to handle and before their roots get intertwined. Water them before you do as this will help them to slip out.

After sowing, cover the seeds by pulling the soil over them with a rake and gently tramping it down with the back of the rake to ensure that the entire seed is in contact with the soil. Rake over the ground where you stood to remove footprints. Label the row at the end.

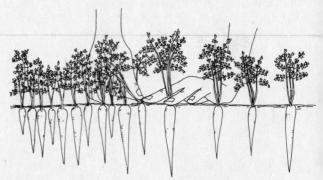

Brassicas and seed-beds

Brassicas are leafy vegetables, members of the cabbage family. If you have the space, raise brassicas on a seed-bed and later transplant them to their permanent quarters. A seed-bed is a much more carefully prepared, small patch of ground, ver firm and finely raked, often with some potting compost added, and without a trace of a weed. If you do not have room for a separate seed-bed, work the brassica ground to just as fine a state before sowing. Or, instead of a seed-bed, you may find it more convenient to buy your brassica plants from a garden centre or nurseryman and just transplant them to your land.

Raising seeds indoors

Seed 'propagation' means raising plants from seed. 'Germination' is the stage between sowing the seed and the arrival of the seedlings.

Many seeds are best sown indoors (or in greenhouses and sometimes cold frames) and later transplanted to their outdoor growing positions. This will help to extend your growing season since hardier vegetables, like peas, lettuces, and cabbage, can get a really flying start by being sown indoors in late winter. Other vegetables prefer a warm start indoors, in anything less than a warm climate, notably cucumbers, marrows, aubergines, peppers, sweet corn and tomatoes. Without it they either will fail to grow at all or only produce a summer crop over a very short time.

The simplest way to propagate seeds is to buy an 'all in one' seed propagating kit, containing seeds, the growing medium, individual peat growing compartments, and a plastic 'greenhouse' top designed to speed up the germination process. The snag is that not many vegetables are sold in such kits, salads and herbs being the most common, and also the pre-packaged nature of them takes a lot of the fun out of growing your own.

On the other hand the most controlled form of propagating unit you can buy, one that has soil warming and/or air-heating cables, thermostatically controlled, is very expensive. It works like a miniature greenhouse.

But there are many other ways of providing

your crops with a cosy start to life. Simple plastic propagators are basically seed-trays covered with a transparent plastic top, usually with a ventilation control which you can open for an hour or so a day to let the seedlings breathe in a change of air. The covers can later be used as cloches on open ground; you can buy these in most areas.

The seed-tray part of the propagating unit can be made out of fruit crates lined with tinfoil or plastic, or large tinfoil pie dishes. These should be used for sowing all small seeds, but larger ones can be planted in yoghurt pots, eggshells (stood upright in an egg box), tins, cardboard milk cartons with their tops cut off, or anything similar, as well as plastic and clay flower pots. You may need to make holes for drainage (cover the holes with crocks, bits of china, flower pots, cups and saucers, or you can use a layer of small stones at the bottom to prevent the soil from blocking, or escaping through the holes). For improvised glasshouse tops use sheets of glass over the flat trays, kitchen plastic or plastic bags fastened round the pots and held up by sticks, jam-jars or plastic cake covers.

Peat pots are popular for seed germination as the seedlings do not have to be lifted out of the pot when they are planted out of doors, or into other, bigger, pots. The whole pot is lowered into the ground and the roots of the plant push their way through the peat and into the surrounding soil. This not only makes it easier for you, but also for the plant, since it avoids the shock of being transplanted. There are also peat pellets on sale which expand when you add water and are made up from specially prepared nutrients so that the seed you plant on the pellet does not even need soil to germinate.

The common way of propagating seeds is as follows:
— Fill your seed trays (or little pots) with seed compost to ½" from the top. (This is different from ordinary compost. It is pre-mixed, specially prepared and sterilized

soil, disease-, pest- and weed-free. Anything that grows in it is what you've
planted.) Immerse the tray in a sink or
bath of water and once the compost is
thoroughly moist allow it to drain.
— Large seeds, like peas and beans, should
be soaked overnight in water and planted
in individual holes 2" apart or put 2 or 3
in each 3" pot. Medium seeds, including
pelleted, can be sown in matchstick or
pencil holes too. Smaller seeds should be
sprinkled evenly all over the surface and
then covered with a *very fine* layer of
compost. Press it down gently.

— Label the containers with their contents
and the date of sowing. Cover them with
glass or seal with polythene and keep
them in a warm, dark place until they
sprout and cover the glass with
newspaper. You must keep the compost
moist, but never soak it. The top of the
central heating boiler, an airing cupboard,
or a fire alcove cupboard are ideal places
to keep seedlings till they germinate. Or
make a 'hot stand' as the diagram shows.

— Take their 'lids' off once a day to allow
the seedlings to breathe (or open the
ventilator holes on your propagator unit),
and wipe away the condensation that
forms on the underside.

When seedlings have germinated, or sprouted,
they will need light. Leave the glass over the
seed-trays till the seedlings touch it but bring
them out into the light. Keep them out of the
sun for the first few days, then put them on a
sunny window-sill. Keep their soil moist all
the time.

As the seedlings begin to crowd each other
thin them, always leaving the strongest looking.
When they are about 2" tall, big enough to
handle by the leaves without risk of damaging
them, lift them out of the seed-trays and transfer
them to small peat pots filled with potting
compost. Or transfer (or 'prick them out') to

another seed-tray, filled with potting compost, and plant them 2" apart. Never use garden soil. Potting compost, like seed compost, is sterilized. It also has an ideal texture for drainage and contains valuable nutrients. Use a standardized proprietary brand (John Innes No. 2 or 3 or a U.S. university standard). Make a hole with a pencil in the compost and plant the seedlings gently up to the level of their leaves. Firm them down and be very careful not to damage the delicate roots. You will not have to prick out pelleted or large seeds that were correctly spaced when you sowed them. Keep them moist. About a week later you can begin to 'harden off' the seedlings if they are going to be planted outside. Hardening off means slowly getting them used to lower temperatures and increased ventilation. Move them to a colder area of the house, then outside for a few warm hours a day, or to a cold frame if you have one.

Transplanting

About a week after hardening off, when all danger of frost has passed and in accordance with the planting-out schedules, your seedlings will be ready to make their final move. By this time they should have at least four or five leaves. If you plan to grow the vegetables indoors the seedlings should be re-potted at this stage because their old pots will not be big enough for their expanding roots, or transfer them to a window-box. If you have more than enough seedlings for the space available, transplant only the sturdiest specimens. Keep the rest for a few days, until those transplanted look as if they have grown accustomed to their new position in life, and then throw them away. Or, of course, compost them.

The methods of transplanting are the same as you will use either for plants that have come from a nursery, or for shifting brassicas from a seed-bed. If you do buy your vegetables from a nursery watch out for, and avoid, wilting, dry, spindly-looking plants and buy only labelled varieties from a reliable and recommended supplier.

Transplant in the early evening, when the soil is not too wet and not too dry. Seeds that have been germinated in 'jiffy' peat pots or pellets are the easiest to transplant. They do not need to be depotted as the peat will decompose in the ground.

If you are transplanting from seed-boxes divide the compost into squares, like cutting a cake, and remove each seedling with a spoon making sure that you take it with a good ball of soil round the roots.

When removing from a pot, hold the pot upside down with the fingers of one hand on either side of the stem of the seedling. Tap the rim of the pot against the edge of a table and the plant will slide out together with a ball of compost.

Milk cartons or yoghurt pots can be cut open with a knife leaving the ball or cube of compost intact.

Make a hole in the ground where the seedling is to go with a dibber or a trowel. It should be large enough for the peat pot or ball of compost to fit comfortably, and the roots of a plant to spread out. If the soil is dry water the hole and allow it to soak in. Lower the seedling into the hole so that the bottom leaves are level with the soil line. Replace the soil round the roots or round the ball of compost and press it down gently but firmly. Water it well and keep the soil moist.

SEED DEPTH AND PLANT DISTANCE GUIDE

	inches		
Artichokes, globe	36	36	½
Artichokes, Jerusalem	20	36	4
Asparagus	18	18	3
Aubergine	24	24	—
Bean, broad	9	9 30*	2
Bean, dwarf french	6	12 24*	2
Bean, runner	12	12 30*	2
Beetroot	6	12	1
Broccoli (sprouting)	18	18	½
Brussels sprouts	24	24	½
Cabbage	20	20	½
Carrots	6	12	½
Cauliflower	24	24	½
Celery and Celeriac	8	14	¼
Chard, Swiss	12	18	½
Chicory	6	12	½
Cucumber	16	24	½
Fennel	8	18	½
Kale	20	20	½
Kohl-rabi	6	15	½
Leeks	6	12	¼
Lettuce and Endive	9	12	½
Marrow	30	30	½
Onion sets	6	12	—
(Shallots)	9	12	—
Parsnips	8	15	1
Peas	4	6* 34*	2
Peppers	18	24	½
Potatoes (earlies)	12	18	6
Radishes	6	9	¼
Salsify and Scorzonera	9	15	½
Spinach	6	12	1
Swede	8	15	½
Sweet Corn	15	30	1
Tomatoes	18	24	½
Turnip	6	15	½
	Final distance between plants in rows	Distance between rows	Depth to sow seed

N.B.: These figures are subject to change with different varieties.

*Refers to
(1) distance between plants in double row.
(2) distance between double row and next row.

If you are transplanting to a larger pot put some compost in the bottom of the new pot, put the seedling in the middle and fill up the sides with more compost. Press down the surface firmly, keeping the soil levels the same. You should always re-pot when the existing one looks simply too small for the plant; sometimes you can see the roots beginning to poke out of the drainage holes at the bottom. Do not try to short-cut the growing processes by starting your seeds off in a big pot and leaving them there all the time. Always start them in a 2"–3" pot, then re-pot to a 5", then a 9" or 10" when the plant becomes pot bound (i.e. when you can hardly see the compost for the roots). For tomatoes, peppers and other vegetables that will need support put the stick in before you transplant as this will avoid the risk of damaging the roots.

EXTENDING THE GROWING SEASON WITH GLASS

You can lengthen your growing season by using glass, and effectively increase the size of your garden and other 'farming' resources. You can get earlier crops before they get anywhere near the shops, and keep on producing into late autumn. You can also grow things like melons, peppers, aubergines and other 'exotics' that simply cannot be grown outdoors if the climate is not warm enough.

Why?

Glass helps to retain heat, to protect plants from the wind, warm up the soil and protect from frost. In cities glass also protects fruit and vegetables from the effects of pollution, and various dog, cat and bird nuisances.

A greenhouse

Will provide the best under-glass growing area of all, but there is unlikely to be space for one in a back garden. Look at some greenhouse brochures and see if you could fit in a small lean-to affair that could double as a sun-lounge. Your balcony may have room for a mini-version too, but you will probably have to make your own out of glass, plastic or perspex. Greenhouses can be heated and can provide you with virtually unlimited scope. Paraffin is the cheapest form of heating to install and run, but you can also get solid-fuel burners, gas and electrical heaters, some thermostatically controlled.

A cold frame

Works like a miniature greenhouse and will usually fit in a small area such as a back yard, balcony or patio. You can make one using wood for the base and old window frames for the top. It should slope so that the rain will run off, and face the south to get the full onslaught of an off-season sun. With soil warming, and perhaps air-heating cables fitted, the frame will be extremely useful.

In general the uses of a cold frame are:
— For propagating seeds (not tender varieties).
— For hardening off (all varieties raised indoors or in heated greenhouses, etc.).
— Crops normally sown in the autumn, such as early cauliflowers or onions, can be over-wintered in the cold frame ready for planting out in the spring.
— Virtually any crop can be advanced by a month or so in the spring, and therefore enjoyed earlier. For example, radishes, lettuces, salad onions, carrots, beets, and so on
— The cold frame can be used to house pots (best to place them on a bed of cinders to help drainage).
— In the summer the cold frame can become home for melons, cucumbers and peppers.

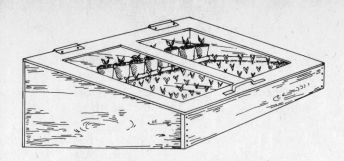

You should ventilate the frame during the day
by propping it open with a stick (except when
the weather is very cold) and close it again at
night. Cover it at night with sacking or an old
rug if there is a danger of frost. In the summer
you may have to whitewash the glass to prevent
the sun scorching the leaves of the plants. Before
planting anything directly in the frame the soil
beneath should be deeply dug, all the weeds
removed and a good layer of potting compost
spread on the surface. If the drainage is likely to
be poor, add some cinders or gravel under the
soil to help the water soak away.

Cloches

Are used to cover rows of vegetables in a garden.
Some are made of glass, others plastic, and a
third type are long polythene tunnels held up

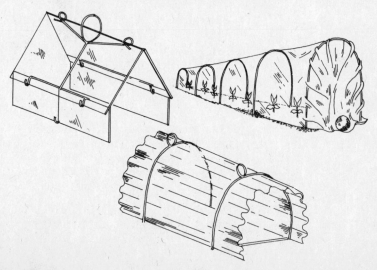

above the plants by wire hoops. If you want to make your own, the polythene type combined with old metal coat hangers would be the easiest, but you can also use plastic propagator covers, see-through umbrellas, old plastic liquid containers with their bottoms cut off, or old aquaria.

Always shut off the ends of a cloche run to prevent draughts. If the weather is hot you can separate the ordinary types of cloche so there are gaps to allow ventilation. If it is very hot you may have to whitewash glass cloches to prevent scorching, just as with the cold frame, or remove the cloches completely during the day. Put the cloches in position at least ten days before planting your vegetables as this will warm the soil in advance. Keep the cloches in position until the leaves begin to touch the underside. In dry weather you may have to lift the cloches to water small plants underneath, but once they grow bigger their roots will reach out far enough into the soil to be able to draw water from either side.

LOOKING AFTER YOUR GARDEN FARM

One of the secrets of successful vegetables is to make them grow as fast as they can, without any check on their progress, almost forcing them through to maturity.

Watering

Watering, regularly and uniformly, is vital to the growing process. Water well, whenever it is dry. An occasional soaking will do your plants more good than a daily sprinkle with a watering-can. The most effective method is to let the water soak into the ground from a hose, rather than to water from overhead or use a sprinkler. In towns, because of the pollution, you should

syringe the leaves on both sides now and then.
If you go off on holiday you must ask someone
to water your crops for you.

Weeding

Your garden would really prefer to be a forest.
Without man's interference the weeds and wild
things would soon take over. But your crops
cannot survive such competition. Hoe away all
weeds as soon as they appear, or pick them out
by hand or with a small fork. If you've planted
your vegetables in a straight line you will be able
to spot the weeds even if you cannot yet identify
them accurately. Keep this weeding up all the
time. If you *must* use proprietary weed killer,
then use a fine rose or a sprinkler bar attachment
on a watering-can and sprinkle between the rows
of crops. The weed killer will destroy only that
part of the plant with which it comes into
contact and does not affect the ground itself.
But another reason for hoeing weeds is that you
should loosen the soil round your crops so that
the air can get to the roots. This is especially
important in dry weather when the surface of

the soil may cake. Hold the hoe at arm's length with the blade horizontal to the surface of the soil. Walk backwards, giving the hoe short pushes just under the surface of the soil as you go. The blade will destroy the weeds and break up the surface.

Between mid-season crops, between a catch crop and its following main crop for example, you should fork over the land to break it up more thoroughly than a hoe can manage. Re-rake the soil before sowing the next crop.

Mulching

A mulch is a ground cover that can be placed everywhere around the plants. It helps to retain moisture in the soil, to eliminate weed competition, and to raise and moderate the temperature of the soil. You can use lots of different material for mulching: black plastic, sacks, rugs, sawdust, tinfoil, stones, newspaper, grass clippings, straw, and so on. If you use an organic mulch, such as peat, leaf mould (add some wood ash to make up for their acidity) or compost, it will decompose and slowly enrich the soil. Don't mulch if the ground is cold (wait until well into the spring), too dry or soaking wet. Water the ground before mulching and keep it away from the base of the plants.

Finally comes your harvest, the end of the life of any fruit or vegetable. Use the charts to guide you, but rely primarily on your eye. Pick them when they look right, when you think they will taste their best; it may be sooner than you think.

Pests and Diseases

Your fruits and vegetables could fall foul of a whole number of pests and diseases. To explain all these doomy possibilities would take a book in itself, and drive any reader to a state of neurotic obsession with the health of the plants, leading to an excessive use of insecticides.

Your crops will be less pest- and disease-prone
when grown on a small scale in town, especially
if you live in an apartment block and out of
pest-flying range. But while nothing will
guarantee their absolute immunity, there are
many preventative steps that you can take before
turning to chemical warfare as the last resort.

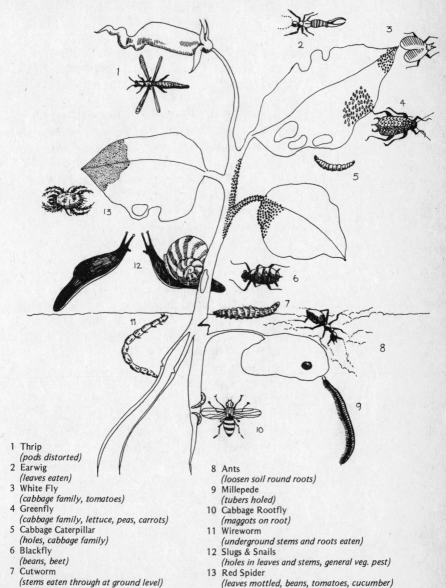

1 Thrip
   (pods distorted)
2 Earwig
   (leaves eaten)
3 White Fly
   (cabbage family, tomatoes)
4 Greenfly
   (cabbage family, lettuce, peas, carrots)
5 Cabbage Caterpillar
   (holes, cabbage family)
6 Blackfly
   (beans, beet)
7 Cutworm
   (stems eaten through at ground level)

8 Ants
   (loosen soil round roots)
9 Millepede
   (tubers holed)
10 Cabbage Rootfly
   (maggots on root)
11 Wireworm
   (underground stems and roots eaten)
12 Slugs & Snails
   (holes in leaves and stems, general veg. pest)
13 Red Spider
   (leaves mottled, beans, tomatoes, cucumber)

In the first place, a nutritious, weed-free and well-cared-for soil will produce strong and healthy plants better able to resist disease when in top physical condition. Many pests only seem to thrive on weaker specimens, too, leaving the healthy looking ones alone. Use sterilized, weed-free potting compost as much as possible, indoors, in window-boxes, balconies, and so on, and build up outdoor soils with plenty of humus-making material. Don't try and economize on space between plants, because overcrowding will weaken their resistance. Water feed and hoe constantly. Mulching will help as well.

Buy pest- and disease-resistant varieties of seed whenever they are available, and always buy a variety suitable for your particular region.

The symptoms you interpret as being caused by pests and diseases may well be the result of your own neglect. Wilting crops, for example, can be caused by poor drainage, insufficient or over-watering, indoor draughts or lack of humidity, gas fumes from the kitchen and rapid changes of temperature, lack of light, or heat, sun scorching, frost, planting outdoors at the wrong time of year for a particular vegetable, overfertilizing, underliming, inadequate rotation of your crops, and so on. Before blaming the bugs make sure that you have not failed your crops in any of these ways.

Not all insects are pests. Some of the most creepy crawly actually do your plants a lot of good: ladybirds will kill off natural predators, earthworms will aerate the soil, and wasps play a crucial role in pollination for example. General insecticides will kill these off. Get in the habit of regularly inspecting your crops, looking for signs of insects especially on the undersides of leaves, and at night because some animals will only come to dine then. Some will be large enough to pick off by hand; others can be scattered with the help of a hard jet of water from a hose. If only one plant in a row has been affected it may be better to pick it from the ground and burn it.

There are many natural preventions and cures to try before reaching for the insecticide. Plant a few aromatic plants in between rows, such as chives, chili peppers, garlic, mint, and even crush some strong smellers and scatter them around, like onion. Cinders or soot barricades will help to keep off slugs, and so will some proprietary baits, slug pellets, that can be positioned well away from your vegetables (they will also keep off cutworms, snails and earwigs).

Always use less harmful sprays and dusting powders, such as pyrethrum and derris, whenever possible, as these will not leave a poisonous residue in the vegetables, but always use in the correct proportion and store them in their original bottles, out of the reach of children. Do not inhale the fumes and always wear rubber gloves. And finally, when you do turn to insecticides, apply them carefully, in the right amount, at the right time, and use the right chemical for the particular disease or pest, rather than the all-purpose poisons. Get advice from a gardening centre or nurseryman, and read all labels carefully.

Some common pests and how to deal with them

In general you should inspect your vegetables and fruits regularly, and at night by torchlight. Look for insects, flies, grubs, eggs, maggots and caterpillars on the leaves, both sides, and the stems as well as the fruit. Look for signs of chewing, discolouring, spots and mottling.

APHIDS:
tiny greenflies, blackflies and other insects. Get rid of them with a hard jet of water from a hose, or use derris/rotenone.

EARWIGS:
proprietary bait; kill when you can

CABBAGE ROOT FLY:
pyrethrum, rotenone

CARROT FLY:
grow carrots early and rapidly

ONION FLY:
calomel dust; grow parsley around vegetables

WHITE FLY:
derris

CATERPILLARS AND MAGGOTS:
great eaters, especially of brassicas. Pick caterpillars off when you see them, dip roots of
brassicas in calomel when transplanting, or dust
with derris.

BIRDS:
can be seed and seedling scavengers, especially
pigeons. Germinate seeds indoors, or cover with
nets (make your own from cotton, and dangle
strips of tinfoil around).

RED SPIDER MITE:
comes when the weather is hot and dry and goes
with derris, rotenone/pyrethrum.

ANTS:
loosen the soil and disturb the roots. Use ant
baits.

THRIPS:
rotenone

EELWORMS, WIREWORMS AND CUTWORMS:
kill the yellow wireworms when you spot them,
use cutworm bait and derris for eelworms.

URBANITES:
such as dogs, cats, children and neighbours, need
good fencing, angry looks and, in the last resort,
bitter complaints.

SLUGS AND SNAILS:
slow but gluttonous, usually at night. Use baits,
slug pellets, but out of pet range, and make a path
of cinders or salt round your patch. Also try
filling an aluminium pie dish with beer and
burying it to ground level. Slugs and snails will
drown in it.

FLEA BEETLE:
derris

U.S. COLORADO BEETLE, CUCUMBER, ASPARAGUS AND BEAN BEETLE:
rotenone

MICE:
don't just eat cheese, so use traps or a soot barrier

MEALY BUGS AND SCALED INSECTS:
soak some cotton wool in methylated spirits, put on the end of a match and rub infected areas.

MILLEPEDES:
not centipedes, which are useful insect eaters, so make sure you count the legs and then murder. Millepedes curl up when touched to save a lot of counting.

AND DISEASES

CLUBROOT:
a swelling on brassica roots that smells awful. Burning is the only cure but liming acid soils and rotation will prevent it. Or calomel.

ROTS, BLIGHTS, DAMPING OFF AND MILDEW:
these white, grey and black patches can be prevented, and sometimes cured, by a dusting with Bordeaux mix. But the original neglect may well be yours, through over watering for example, especially during wet summers. Many varieties are sold resistant to these sorts of diseases, so buy them whenever you can. Indoors you should always use sterilized composts and make sure your crops are well ventilated.

POTATO WART:
grows on tubers and stems, can be prevented by buying resistant varieties.

PARSNIP CANKER:
produces dark patches on top of the root, but is unlikely to occur with Avonresister variety.

CELERY LEAF SPOT:
prevent by buying resistant varieties or use Bordeaux mix.

GROWING FRUIT AND VEGETABLES WHEN YOU DON'T OWN ANY LAND

Allotments

If you don't have a back-garden, try to get an allotment, either through a local authority, a private allotment association or even organisations such as the railways who have tracts of unused land. The chances are that there will be a waiting list, as their popularity is increasing all the time. Their average size is 90' by 30' and the cost of renting such a grand potential plot is a nominal pound or two a year. You may have to put a lot of work in when you first take over an allotment — weeding, digging and generally building up the quality of the soil. For the first year you could grow potatoes, cabbages and Brussels sprouts, as they grow vigorously and will help you to come to terms with the weeds. Although an allotment will never be as conveniently located as your own back yard you will have all the land resources you'll need for an all-the-year-round supply of vegetables for a small family. But that will take quite a bit of effort on your part.

Other people's gardens

If you can't get an allotment you might be able to use somebody else's land in return for giving them a share of the fruits and vegetables that you grow there. Many town gardens are weed museums and it would be well worth a few door-to-door approaches to see what you can get. Or place an advertisement in a local news-paper. Old people, especially those who cared for their gardens when they were physically more active, might welcome a re-awakening of their soil and the enjoyment of plenty of fresh and free food in return.

But you don't really need any land at all in order to grow your own fruits and vegetables. Indoor seed propagation is only the tip of the iceberg as far as your indoor growing potential is concerned.

Window-boxes

Perhaps the most obviously neglected growing area for the apartment bound city slicker is the window-sill. Lots of vegetables like lettuces, spring onions, carrots and tomatoes, are not deep rooting and are perfectly suited to window-box culture, but you must buy the small varieties from the seed catalogues. Herbs are a perfect choice too.

Gardening centres sell a wide range of window-boxes, ready made from plastic, polystyrene, fibreglass and wood. If you are at all craft-minded, the advantage of making your own is that it can be tailored to the size of your window-sill. Use 1" thick hardwood, 9" deep, and join the sections together with brass corner brackets and screws. Drill ½" drainage holes every 6" (or better still burn them through with a red-hot poker as burnt wood is more water

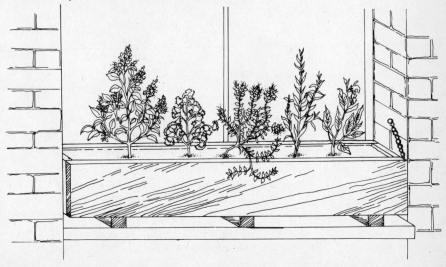

resistant). Fix two or three wedge-shaped blocks to the bottom of the box and add handles at either end. Coat the timber with a non-creosote preservative or, if you feel like a real baptism by fire, paint the inside of the box with paraffin, set it alight and turn it upside down after a minute or two. Better do that outside the house!

Secure the window-box to the wall with brackets, hook and eye screws, or a small chain at either end. When filled with compost the box will be extremely heavy and could cause a disaster if it were to be blown off in a strong wind. Nor do people below care to have dirty drainage water dripping on their heads, so try and use trays underneath if you can get them to fit.

Crock the drainage holes or cover the base with a layer of small pebbles, then fill the box with potting compost to within an inch of the top. Sow or plant your vegetables or herbs — it is probably best to propagate indoors and transplant the seedlings to the box. Or you could just fill the box with a row of pots resting on a layer of pebbles. The laziest of growers could just erect a plank frontage across the window to disguise and retain the pots.

You can 'greenhouse' your window-box, or hopefully boxes, with jam-jars over the seedlings after transplanting, or cloche them with a section of corrugated plastic or polythene, with the ends sealed off. Of course, if you are using pots, you can cover them with plastic bags as already described. If you don't greenhouse your box at least protect seedlings from hungry birds by stretching some black cotton between wooden stakes pushed into the compost at either end.

Don't neglect the inside window-sill area as this will be very light, and possibly sunny. Some manufactured window-boxes are in fact dual purpose and can be made to fit inside or out. Runner beans, with their scarlet flowers, and other climbers will make an excellent curtain if they are trained up lengths of bamboo, secured to the sides of the box.

Balconies, patios and roofs

Window-box structures are ideal for balconies, both secured to wide balcony ledges, and for constructing a tiered growing area along the sides. The light on balconies is likely to be very bright and will reach most of your growing areas. You can also hang window-boxes outside balconies, on the city side of the wall or railings. Needless to say they should be securely hung and drip proof.

Balconies can be home to all manner of containers, including larger pots, tubs and boxes (see p. 60), which should be raised off the ground slightly, by jam-jar lids, say, so that surplus water can drain away. This in turn should be able to drain off the balcony rather than into your living-room. The largest tubs can be stood on home-made castor platforms to enable them to be wheeled about.

If you have jungle plans for your balcony, involving a hefty volume of soil, you'd better check with the borough engineer or an architect to be sure that the structure will bear the weight.

Although balconies receive plenty of air and

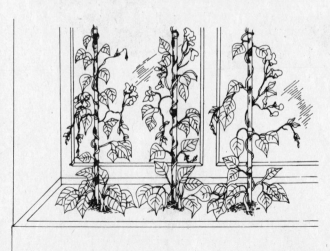

light they are also vulnerable to wind. Protect your vegetables with plastic sheeting or some other form of screening, perhaps climbing varieties like cucumbers, peas and beans, or both so that the plastic has a partial greenhouse effect on the vegetables behind it. Make sure they don't touch each other, though, or the vegetables will get prematurely fried. Climbers can also be trained up balcony railings as an added protection against the wind, or up unsightly drainpipes. What about a vine, if your climate is fairly mild? To start off other warm-climate crops you could build a cold frame at one end, or make a plastic lean-to greenhouse.

Patios, terraces, verandahs or whatever else you may chose to call a small outdoor extension to your home are all suitable areas for growing food. The ways of adapting them to serve this end are unlimited. Your home may have access to roof space too, but here a specialist's advice should definitely be taken before you burden the structure with more than it was perhaps meant to take. If you are thinking of anything heavier than a few pots it will probably need strengthening. You will also have the problems and expense of protection from prevailing winds, drainage, getting soil or sedge peat up there, at least 9" deep, and retaining walls to prevent the soil being swept down to street level again; also people falling likewise as they take a step back to admire your prize marrows. And then there are the temperature extremes that roof gardens fall victim to, the heavy watering programme needed because of their rapid drying out and maybe the problem of tricky access. In many ways a roof garden, if you have the potential, is the most realistic alternative that a city dweller has to a back-garden, but don't underestimate the scale of the conversion job involved.

Patios and roof areas are more easily equipped with tubs, boxes or larger containers, and raised beds of compost, than converted into gardens in their own right. All short-rooted vegetables can be grown in attractively shaped, 6" to 9" deep containers, rather like giant window-boxes. They can be made in different sizes and arranged in different layouts to suit the general design of your outdoor area. Raised beds are even grander and, filled with potting compost, will produce some excellent crops and are less back-breaking to look after than a garden at soil level. You can in fact build them in a garden over a layer of poorer soil to save you the struggle of trying to improve the existing land. Make them from at least 9" wide planks, securely and tightly bracketed at the corners, and drill holes along the sides at the bottom for any surplus water to drain away. Paint the wood in non-creosote preservative, and then in bright colours if you fancy. Line the bottom with pebbles or cinders and then top it up with potting compost. The compost will be expensive but over many months of fresh, wholesome vegetable eating, the cost will be worth it. And think of the basic spade work and

soil improvement effort that you will be spared.
One final point for those adjacent farming
patches; paint any surrounding walls white, as
this will reflect the heat and light to where it is
most wanted, and *use* them to grow things on.
When you first consider your growing resources,
look up as well as down.

GROWING INDOORS

Most fruits and vegetables, like all plants, need
plenty of light, humidity, water, freedom from
draughts (such as opening and closing windows)
and non-fluctuating temperatures in order to
grow. Greenhouse crops, like tomatoes,
aubergines, peppers, as well as lettuce, are most
suitable for growing in sunny lounges or those
glass-sided home extensions.

But all upper-storey, one-floor dwellings have
windows, lots of them, and some will get plenty
of sun. The actual window-sill, both inside and
out, will only offer a one-level spread per
window but you could build two or three shelves
that fit right across the window on the inside,
perhaps using glass, to house pots. If there are
small children about it might be safer to cut
holes in a wooden shelf for the pots to fit in.
Line the hole with a polythene 'cup' to prevent
water dripping on to the floor. If your bank of
vegetables or herbs helps to block the view of

nosey neighbours, or your vision of the gasworks, so much the better.

Climbing plants make excellent room dividers, provided that they get plenty of sunshine, and vegetables can be just as pleasant to look at as familiar house plants. Fix bamboo sticks from floor to ceiling, or just let the climbers roam over an existing bookshelf type of room-divider unit.

Use as many rooms as you can for growing things. Bathrooms, for example, are usually neglected, but are often full of light and generally have a higher humidity level than the rest of the flat. But beware of temperature extremes, especially in the kitchen where the temperature tends to fluctuate and also cooking fumes may not suit your crops.

In the office

If you spend your working days in an office, take another look at it from an urban farming view-point. What about those window-sills, if you can actually open the windows of your concrete glasshouse? Or the inside areas, in front of the window? It is easy to grow a much healthier lunch than the usual hamburger and chips or processed cheese sandwich that you normally relish. How about a constant supply of alfalfa to garnish any sandwich with flavour and valuable protein that can be grown in your desk drawer? (See page 57).

Switched-on sunshine

If your home is short on sun, or you want to grow some food in dim corners, perhaps in a shelf unit or even a closet cupboard, use artificial lights. They will produce year-round vegetables, or the luxury of winter salads.

You can use ordinary fluorescent lights, preferably in units of two 40-watt bulbs, or better still buy fluorescent tubes that are specially designed for indoor growing. The

brightness of ordinary lights can be checked with a photographic light meter to compare with outside light. Mount both sorts of light in reflectors (make them from tin foil glued on to stiff card) fixed just above the plants.

You can buy, or again make, multi-tiered tray stands with light fittings underneath each shelf shining on to the shelf below. Some are combined with a base heater unit. They make excellent propagators for your new year's supply of food.

It is important to follow the instructions that come with the lights regarding distance from the plants and their watering requirements. Use a twenty-four-hour on/off electrical timer so that you don't have to remember.

Radishes, lettuces, beets, sweet baby carrots, onions, leeks, parsley and many other mini varieties of vegetables will flourish under artificial lights.

Growing in the dark - mushrooms

Mushrooms do not care about the light and can be grown in cellars, attics, sheds, cupboards under the stairs, garages, junk closets, almost anywhere. They can be grown all the year round provided that the temperature stays cool, around 50° to 60°F, and there are no draughts (but there should be ventilation). They will also grow in a sink cupboard, or even under your bed.

Buy sterilized compost and mushroom spawn, often sold in pre-packaged units, pre-sown, with full instructions. All you have to do with the pre-packaged kits is to keep them moist, but never soaking. There will be no smell or mess. With the do-it-yourself version you simply sprinkle the spawn over the compost and work it slightly under the surface. After about four weeks, while the mushrooms are white and still closed, you will be able to start picking them.

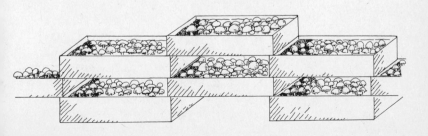

Twist them out carefully and remove any bits that are left as these could ruin those unpicked.

Grow your mushrooms in old fruit or fish boxes lined with polythene, or seed-trays. If you want to produce them on a large scale, stack the boxes as the diagram shows. Or use an old three-tiered tea trolley. Don't under-estimate their yield — one square foot will produce about a pound of mushrooms.

And in those gloomy indoor areas don't forget to reserve space for germinating your seeds. They will, of course, need to be kept much warmer than mushrooms.

OTHER DIM SOULS SPROUTING VEGETABLES

These can be grown at any time of the year and do not need sunshine. They are childishly simple to produce.

Mustard and cress has been an indoor growing favourite for a long time. Place a few layers of blotting paper, a flannel, a J cloth, or a tea-cloth, in a pie dish (or similar) and keep it moist.

Sprinkle the cress seeds on the surface and then do the same with the mustard seeds on another dish a few days later (they take less time to mature). Both will be ready to eat in about two weeks and only need to see the light once they are a flourishing growth.

Chinese-restaurant-type Mung bean shoots can be grown even in a drawer, in a similar way to mustard and cress. They have an extremely high food value and a rich vitamin content just after the seeds have germinated, and can be eaten raw, in salads, quick fried, or boiled for two minutes. Sprout them in the same way as mustard and cress but soak them first overnight. Slide their growing tray into a polythene bag to retain moisture and keep them in any warm dark place. Eat when they are about 1½" long, a few days after germination.

Alfalfa (or lucerne) is the third important and easy to grow sprouting vegetable, again rich in protein — half a cup of alfalfa is the equivalent in vitamin C of six glasses of pure orange juice. You can grow it in the same way as mustard and cress, or in a jar. For the latter, wash the seeds, put four teaspoonfuls into a jar, and then half fill with tepid water. Shake it, drain it, and cover the top with muslin, secured with an elastic band. Keep the jar on its side in a warm place — like a drawer — (with a temperature around 65° to 70°). Every morning, noon and evening half fill the jar with water and drain. The shoots will be ready to eat in three to five days. Rinse them in cold water before eating.

Other sprouting foods are: fenugreek, adzuki beans, triticale, lentils, chick-peas, sunflower seeds, wheat, peas, radishes, fennel, celery seeds — ask for sprouting, not sowing, seeds.

Hydroponics, or growing plants without soil

After their germination stage, plants need soil to grow in because from it they not only get support, enabling them to stand up straight, but also the nutrients or foods that they need to live on. Having seen how you can grow vegetables without natural sunshine, you can now experiment with a method of growing without soil, known as hydroponics. The plants are supported by an alternative aggregate, such as sand, and they are fed on a solution of water and mineral salts, which they would normally draw from the earth.

The science of hydroponics has had its greatest impact on food growing in developing countries where barren, infertile land has been made productive. But the techniques, on a much smaller scale, are also of relevance to the urban farmer. It is a more exact and controlled way to grow things, and there is no risk of your vegetables suffering from soil-borne pests and diseases. Here's how to do it.

For a container you can use an old kitchen sink, a large bowl, a wooden box lined with heavy-duty polythene, plastic troughs, big tins or pots, or bricks and roofing felt. Make three or four drainage holes, preferably at one end, and raise the other slightly. Make plugs for the drainage holes out of cork or Plasticine.

You can buy ready made mixtures of fertilizer salts containing the proper nutrients (like phostrogen and sustanum), for sustaining your vegetable growth, from gardening centres (or see the addresses at the end of the book). You must dissolve them in the correct amount of water, and keep the aggregate in the containers always moist with the solution. Follow the chemical manufacturer's instructions for the exact mixing ratio and frequency of watering.

The aggregate should be light, sterile and porous, such as coarse sand, vermiculite, gravel, small pebbles, cinders (soaked and washed) or broken bricks. Put broken flower pots or larger pebbles over the drainage holes to prevent them getting blocked or the aggregate seeping out. Thoroughly wet the aggregate, draining it in a sink or bath, or outside, and then replace the plugs.

Once you have watered the aggregate with plain water, sow the seeds just as you normally would. Water lightly again, still using plain water, and then 24 hours later give the plants their first feed with the nutrient solution. After that keep the growing aggregate constantly moist, but never soaking.

Every few days remove the plugs and allow any surplus water or solution in the bottom of the container to drain out (into saucers or aluminium pie trays) for two or three hours. Re-plug and re-feed. Once every ten days repeat this but wash out the aggregate with plain water, and change the solution.

Keep the growing units warm, ventilated (but out of draughts), near the window at all times of the year. The growing procedures, regarding thinning, transplanting, and so on, are exactly the same as for any other plant. Occasionally wipe the leaves with a damp sponge, and rake over the aggregate with a kitchen fork. With hydroponics you do not have to rotate your crops, just clean the aggregate thoroughly at the end of the year. And you can grow any vegetables or salads you like, without digging, weeding, hard work or seasons to worry about.

You can build a simple natural gravity-feed system instead of using the watering-can method of feeding. A bucket is attached to the bottom of the tank or container with a rubber hose and raised to fill the tank and lowered to drain it, as the diagram shows. Cover the bucket to prevent evaporation, and change the solution every two weeks.

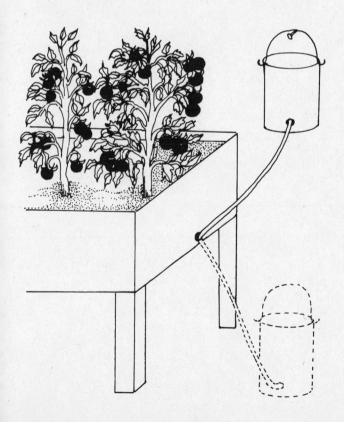

Hydroponic units can also be used with automatic watering devices (see p. 73), especially when you want to go away on holiday. Whether you choose the capillary or gravity system you should mix the minerals in the water reservoir in the correct proportions. When you return from your holiday let the units drain completely, for a day or two wash the aggregate out with plain water, replace plugs and re-feed with fresh nutrients.

SOME IDEAS FOR INDOOR FRUIT AND VEGETABLE CONTAINERS

Improvised and recycled

Tins, painted, especially big canteen or restaurant cans; oil cans; stone sinks; ceramic bathroom fittings; half a car tyre; photographic trays; chamber pots; chimney pots; carpet tubes; wicker laundry hamper (with plastic liner); milk cartons; ice-cube trays; an aquarium; bricks and roofing felt; drainpipes; kitchen catering equipment (pans, etc.); cut-down detergent bottles; a supermarket trolley (with plastic liner); buckets & waste-paper baskets; concrete breeze blocks.

Home-made

Wooden troughs or plastic window-boxes joined together and made into a table for display (perhaps with a light fitting); hanging baskets made from old wire or glass lampshades (line wire frames with green polythene or moss); invisible pot hangers made from perspex and hung up by fishing line; rope or leather (macramé) pot holders (with a saucer under pot); big boxes and converted tea chests; wire ring holders that will hold pots on to railings.

Conventional

Flower pots (use the plastic ones and stand in saucers or tin foil pie tins); pole plant stands; wall brackets to hold flower pots on walls, inside and out; hanging baskets, non-drip with welded watering saucers; tubs, pots, urns; multiple plant pots (for herbs) and strawberry pots; grow bags (see later).

Always use potting compost and change it every two years. Drainage is very important. If the soil remains too wet the roots of the plant will rot. But you can't always make holes in containers — big ceramic pots or stone sinks, for example. In these cases cover the bottom quarter with a layer of gravel, small stones and charcoal before adding the compost, and always take care not to overwater.

What to grow without a garden

The simple answer is virtually anything you want. There is no point in trying to produce space-consuming roots indoors, and whatever you do want to grow choose the small, the 'Tiny Tim', 'Tom Thumb', stump-rooted, compact, dwarf varieties. And be adventurous.

Here are a few suggestions, but don't let them restrict your own ideas:

HERBS:
these are ideal for growing indoors since they don't take up much space and can be grown on a sunny window-sill. If they are outside the kitchen window all you have to do is lean out, snip and pop them into your dishes. Dry them if they are in abundance, and give them away as presents (see page 65).

MUSHROOMS:
will grow where other things won't, so are perfect for the indoor gardener (see page 55).

SPROUTING VEG:
alfalfa, mung beans and mustard and cress. They
can fit into any odd corner. In relation to the
space they take up their vitamin value is
incredibly high (see page 56).

SALADS:
another choice for the window-box. Small varieties
of lettuces, carrots, radishes and onions take up
little compost room.

CLIMBERS:
peas and beans are best suited to outside balconies
or for training up walls. Their pretty flowers make
an attractive screen. Try growing them indoors as
room dividers, up bamboo or trellis, but only in
sunny areas. There are also dwarf varieties that
support themselves, or you can pinch their
growing tips when they get as tall as you want them
to.

MELONS:
canteloupes can be grown on a sheltered balcony,
against a sunny wall, and with some clear plastic
in front of it (but not touching it or the melons
will scorch). They can also be grown in a very
sunny bay window or sun lounge (see page 147).

MARROWS:
and courgettes and cucumbers; need a deep soil
and so should be grown in tubs or deep pots and
allowed to trail.over the side. Or grow them in
deep hanging baskets in a sunny window and they
will cascade down. They must be kept in the sun
and watered well, and you must assist in their
pollination (see under 'marrows' in individual
vegetable section).

STRAWBERRIES:
you can buy strawberry pots specially designed
for the smaller alpine strawberry (the same pots
can also be used to grow herbs), or grow them
from hanging baskets. Fill the container to the
openings with compost, put a plant or cutting
in each hole so that it is sticking out of the
sides, then add some more compost, more plants,

and finally a collection at the top. Keep in a fairly sunny spot.

TOMATOES:

these are easiest to grow in grow bags, polythene sacks filled with peat that has all the necessary plant foods added in the right proportions. They dispense with the need for pots and can be used anywhere — even commercial tomato growers have begun to use them on a mass scale. To use them simply cut up, fold as the instructions tell you, and plant (they can also be used for aubergines and peppers, cucumbers, in fact anything you like that is not too deep rooting).

Without grow bags you can produce tomatoes indoors like this: sow the seeds thinly in seed-trays in the early spring (and propagate as usual) or buy good bedding plants from a nurseryman (or grow from pre-planted tomato kits). Restrict to one main shoot and pinch out all side shoots. Eventually transplant to a 10" pot and tie the plant to a cane. Keep in a sunny, warm, airy place and stand the pots on a tray of wet pebbles to provide a moist atmosphere. Tap the stalks each day to help pollination (or shake the plant gently). (See page 137).

GROW BAG

Cherry tomatoes can be grown from hanging baskets; they trail down as the fruits grow, and pixie tomatoes are suitable for window-boxes.

PEPPERS AND AUBERGINES:
both can be pot raised indoors, in compost, and kept in a warm, sunny spot, free from draughts. Peppers can also be trained to trail from hanging baskets.

You will get further ideas for your 'gardenless farm' in the sections on individual fruits and vegetables.

Growing your own herbs

Herbs were first introduced into Britain by the Romans, but it was in the sixteenth century that they became widely popular. The herb garden at Kew, with its scores of different herbs, is a classic example of the Elizabethan enthusiasm for the plants.

Herbs have been grown as decorative plants, for medicinal reasons, for their aromatic qualities, for face and body preparations and above all for their culinary uses, for flavouring and garnishing dishes, as well as helping rich acidy foods get digested without pain or embarrassment.

Since most herbs flourish naturally in sunny, dry climates, like the Mediterranean countries, so they like to grow in sunny spots in the city, sheltered from strong winds, and on a well drained soil. But they are not hard to grow and are an excellent choice for window-box farmers, as well as those with a patio, backyard and other outdoor, or indoor, places for them to flourish. The nearer they are to the kitchen, so the more accessible they will be to your cooking operations, and herbs flourish best when they are being constantly used.

You can buy a pre-packaged herb garden kit, from chain stores, that contains ready-planted herb seeds under a plastic dome cover which acts as a mini-greenhouse and helps germination. Just moisten the pots and place them on a sunny window-sill. Thin out the shoots as they grow and then transplant each peat pot to a clay pot, well crocked to ensure good drainage and filled with potting compost.

Another easy growing method is to buy perennials as seedlings from a nursery. Most herbs are perennials and have to be replaced every third year, at which time you can also renew the soil they grow in. Many can be grown from seeds or cuttings. Annuals are usually grown from seed, planted ¼" deep and raised just like vegetables (in the warm and dark till they germinate) and later transferred to pots or the window-box, or directly outdoors, about 6" apart.

Keep their soil or potting compost fairly moist and occasionally feed them a little liquid manure. Indoor herbs like an even temperature with sun (although some don't mind partial shade). Pinch out the flowers to promote leaf growth. Better to harvest them before they flower and, for the best flavour, do so in the morning, before the sun hits them but after the dew has dried. To pick them pinch back from the top. Herbs can be used fresh or dry (see the section on storage). Either way they should be used constantly as they grow best under pressure.

The guide on page 70 is a list of the most useful and easily grown herbs for the town dweller. Don't bother to grow all of them, and feel free to substitute your own favourites. If you have lots of space, for example, you might like to plant a dwarf bay tree in a large tub on your patio or directly in the garden. If you enjoy pickles, then dill should feature in your herb selection. And don't neglect the wild things: the wild mint, sorrel and nettles for soups; dandelions and tamer nasturtiums for salads, which need not take up your valuable space since they are usually in such general abundance anyway.

- to make a herb tea use two cups of boiling water poured over two teaspoonfuls of the herbs and allow it to draw for five minutes. Strain it and sweeten it.
- to make a bouquet garni you need 2 sprigs of parsley, 2 sprigs of thyme, 2 stems of celery, 1 sprig of majoram, 1 sprig of rosemary and 1 bay leaf, all tied in a piece of cheesecloth.
- mixed herbs consist of sage, parsley, thyme and tarragon.
- *fine herbes* are made up from dried tarragon, chives, chervil, parsley, all finely chopped in equal proportions, blended together and used on omelettes, grilled chicken, fish and vegetables generally.
- to make tarragon vinegar you must pick the leafy stalks of tarragon and put them in a tall glass jar. Fill with white or cider vinegar, screw on the lid and leave it in a sunny place for two weeks. Strain the vinegar into a bottle and leave the tarragon behind. Add a clove of garlic and perhaps a piece of chili pepper with the tarragon if you want to.
- to make hot herb bread you will need the equivalent of a cup of butter, 1 tbsp. of chopped dried parsley, 1 tsp. finely chopped garlic, ½ tsp. of thyme, pinch of marjoram and long French loaf. Soften, but do not melt, the butter and work in the herbs with a wooden spoon. Slice through the bread just to the bottom crust and butter one side of each slice with herb butter. Wrap the loaf tightly in tinfoil and heat in a medium oven for fifteen minutes. Serve hot.

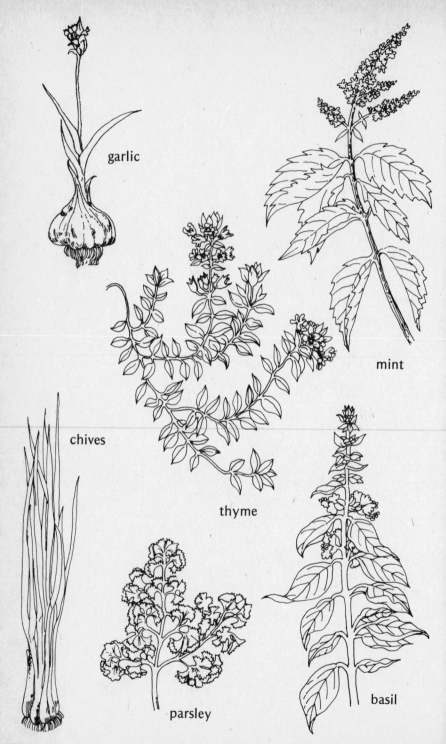

garlic

mint

chives

thyme

parsley

basil

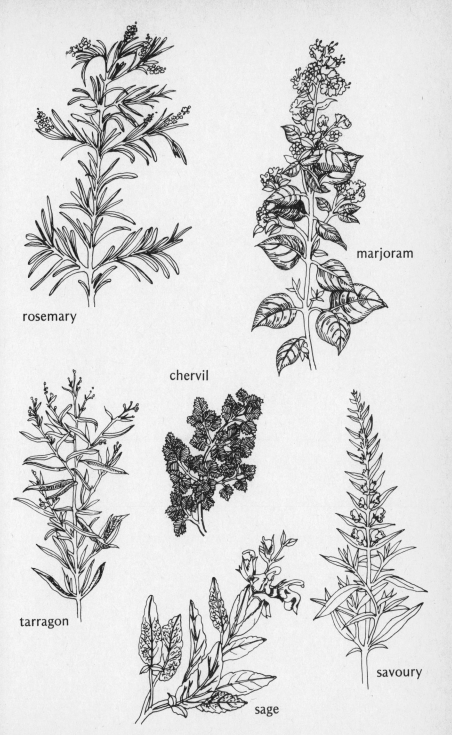

rosemary

marjoram

chervil

tarragon

sage

savoury

A GUIDE TO HERBS

	General growing points	What to use it with (I) dishes	(II) particular vegetables
CHIVES *perennial*	A member of the onion family but grown for its stalks. Plant tiny bulbs or seeds in the spring. Use often. Pretty.	Chives have the flavour of mild onion. Goes well with scrambled eggs and salads. Make chives butter for grilled meat.	Corn, potatoes, tomatoes
THYME *perennial*	Lots of different varieties. Grow from seeds (or cuttings) in early spring. Cut back the growing tips to keep bushy.	Strong tasting, with cottage and cream cheese and sea food cocktails and stuffings. Make thyme tea mixed with honey, for sore throats and colds.	Turnips, broccoli, aubergine, beets, carrots, leeks, onions.
MARJORAM *perennial*	English equivalent of oregano. Smells nice. Grow from seeds (or cuttings) and remove blooms when they appear.	Pizza and tomato-based pasta sauces and salads. Also for meats generally, especially sausages and stews, and stuffings. Teas for mild stomach upsets and bad breath.	Cauliflower, courgettes, peas, mushrooms, cooked celery, potatoes, tomatoes, spinach, aubergine, greens, carrots.
SWEET BASIL *annual*	A bushy plant that likes the sunniest position. Grow from seed, early spring. Pinch buds to prevent seed setting.	Pasta sauces and stews, as well as salads and cheese dishes. Antiseptic for bites and stings.	Beans, peas, carrots, tomatoes, turnips, mushrooms, marrow and vegetable soups.
TARRAGON *perennial*	Another good smeller. Grow from cuttings or seeds in early spring.	A versatile herb that can be used with chicken dishes, in various sauces and stuffings, with eggs, avocado pear and ham-burgers. And it induces sleep.	Asparagus, beets, cabbage, potatoes, tomatoes, peas, mushrooms.
MINT *perennial*	Many types (spear/pepper) grow from mint cuttings, planted 2" apart and thin it by using it. Easier to grow than stop. Strong smelling.	Mint sauce (for lamb and veal). Base for kebab marinades. Ice cream. Mint julep — with brandy, sugar and ice. Mint tea, good for sore mouths and remember-ing a Moroccan holiday.	Carrots, peas, beans and potatoes.
PARSLEY *biennial, perennial*	Grow from seed in the early spring — slow to germinate. Pinch off the growing blooms.	Parsley sauce, of course, on fish, (just parsley and white sauce). Also for salads, eggs, vinaigrette sauce, etc. Rich in vitamins A and C.	Peas, artichokes, corn,, turnips, mushrooms, potatoes, tomatoes and vegetable soups.
ROSEMARY *perennial*	Plant rosemary from a cutting in the late summer. Pale-blue flowers in the spring.	A strong-tasting herb used best in strong-tasting foods, like game, minestrone, strong fish, roast lamb. Reputed to cure insomnia.	Cauliflower, peas, spinach, cabbage and turnips.
GARLIC *perennial*	Strictly an onion, not a herb. Plant a clove in the early spring. Lift bulbs when leaves die, at end of summer.	Use gently to flavour stews and casseroles. Rub fondue and salad bowls with it before their preparation. Pickles. Good for general health and ant bites.	String in bunches like onions.
SUMMER SAVOURY *annual*	Easy to grow, from seed, in the early spring. Aromatic.	Use in salads, sandwiches and egg dishes.	Beans, cauliflower, cabbage, marrow and artichokes.
SAGE *perennial*	Grow from cuttings or seeds in the early spring.	Another strong taster that should be used sparingly in stuffings, pâtés, sausages, roast meats, plus eggs and cheese. Sage tea for gargling and after shock.	Aubergine, onions, stuffings for all vegetables.
CHERVIL *annual*	Simple to grow, from seeds sown at four-week intervals from March to August.	Soups, salads, eggs and fish dishes.	Beets, cucumber, lettuce, potatoes, tomatoes, salads generally.

How to grow
your own yoghurt

Not a fruit, nor a vegetable, but something you
can grow nevertheless. To make two quarts of
live yoghurt you will need fresh milk (pasteurized
or not), yoghurt culture (3 heaped tablespoons —
you can get it from most health food stores), 2
quart jars (with lids), a dairy thermometer (useful
but not vital), and a large pot, deeper than the
yoghurt jars and preferably one with a lid.
    Warm the milk to 112° F (100° F to 120° F
will do) and heat up the water in the pot to the
same temperature. Pour the yoghurt culture into
the milk and stir well with a wooden spoon, then
pour the mixture into the jars, and put them into
the pot and put the lids on, but not tightly. Put
the jars in the pot so that the heated water
reaches the necks of the jars, and cover the pot.
Keep the pot on the stove and maintain the same
temperature for three or four hours. Do not
disturb the jars in any way. Instead of using the
stove you could add hot water to the old as the
temperature drops and wrap towels round the pot
to conserve the heat, again taking care not to jog
the yoghurt.
    Remove the jars from the pot, cool and
refrigerate. Save some of the yoghurt to start the
next batch and keep your supplies going in this
way. Eat all the rest with fresh, home-grown
fruits, wheat germ and nuts.

The general care of indoor fruits and vegetables

Indoor plants are usually overwatered, running the risk of root rot, whereas outdoor plants tend not to be watered sufficiently to reach their roots. The compost should always be kept moist, but never soaked. No two fruits or vegetables will be alike in their watering needs, which will also vary according to size, light, temperature, climate, season and their stage of development. To test for dryness touch the surface with your finger, or put a piece of newspaper flat on the surface and see if it absorbs any moisture, or, to be really safe, use a moisture meter.

Use tepid water (do you like cold showers?) and water at dusk to prevent the loss due to evaporation. Never put plants straight into the sun after watering, as they might get scorched. During summer months you may well find that you have to water your indoor crops twice a day. Use a fine rose watering-can attachment on seedlings (if you are using a watering-can) or you can fill the bath or sink and stand the containers in water. Occasionally use a fine mist spray on the leaves and if your neighbourhood suffers from heavy pollution, wipe the leaves with a damp piece of cheesecloth.

In centrally heated flats you should have a humidifier on each radiator, or stand the vegetables above a supply of water. Smaller pots and containers can be stood on a dish of pebbles which are kept wet — the evaporation of water from their surfaces will keep the area around the plants high in humidity.

Indoor fruits and vegetables like an occasional feed of liquid fertilizer, but don't overdo it. The odd flick of cigarette ash, or washed and dried tea and coffee grounds will also benefit your crops.

Break up the surface of the soil round your indoor vegetables with a fork every two or three weeks, but mind the roots. This will aerate the soil. Keep the plants out of draughts.

Many pollinating insects, like bees and moths, can't manage the flight up to high-rise flats. Your crops will be less disease- and pest-prone, but to overcome the pollination problem you should tap the stems of some plants, like tomatoes, and give others an overhead watering with a fine rose, or dust their flowers with a camel-hair brush, feather-duster or feather.

Going away on holiday

Your fruits and vegetables should be all right for about a week indoors without watering, provided that you water them really well before leaving. Cover big plants with polythene dry cleaners bags supported by sticks and tied round the bottom and they will stay moist for over two weeks. You can also mulch plants with marble chips to hold the water in.

Automatic watering methods are useful both for holidays and if you have a bad memory. There are two basic techniques:
— wick: one end placed in the soil and one end in water and as the roots draw water from the soil round the roots it is replaced by capillary action. All you have to do is keep the reservoir topped up or, if you want an even more automated system, link the reservoir to your mains supply via a plastic tank with a ball valve. The wick can be made of cloth, an ordinary lamp wick, or use special fibre matting.
— you can siphon water from a trough, changing the rate of drip by raising or lowering the slope of the tube. There are more elaborate versions of this method that can be used on balconies, greenhouses, in fact anywhere, providing you connect them to the mains water supply.

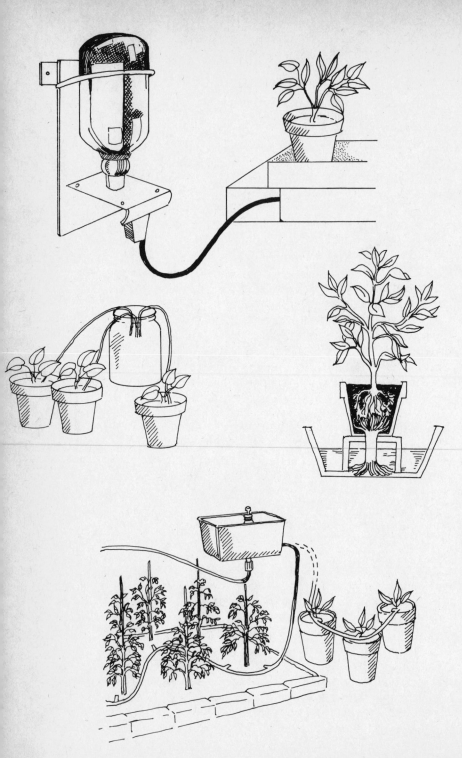

Children and growing things

Children will derive plenty of enjoyment from
your urban farming activities, especially if you
structure one or two things around them or can
afford to give them a patch of their own, even
just a single window-box, to grow things in.
Your climbing beans, for example, could easily
climb up and around a pole wigwam. Set five or
six poles in a circle and tie them together at the
top. Then bind wire or string round, from the
bottom to the top. Other climbing plants can
be built round a three-sided hideaway.

Indoors, children can grow mustard and cress,
or onion or garlic flowers, by planting the bulbs
in potting compost, just like ordinary bulbs.

Fruit pips and stones (such as orange, lemon,
grapefruit, melon, cherry and grape) can be grown
easily. Soak them overnight and plant two or
three in each pot filled with potting compost.
Use yoghurt pots with a hole made in the bottom
and crocked with a few stones. Stand them in
saucers and keep the compost moist. Keep them
warm and out of the light until they sprout.

To grow a carrot plant, cut off the top inch
and place it on some small stones in a bowl. Use
other stones to hold it in place and keep the
level of water always to the level of the carrot
top. Keep it in the sunlight. Pineapple tops can
also be 'turned' into plants by putting them in
compost (so can beets, parsnips and turnips).
Carrot plants can also grow upside down. Cut
off the top two inches, hollow out the middle
for a water reservoir, push cocktail sticks through
the sides and hang it so that it will trail down.

To grow potato plants, push four cocktail
sticks into a potato so that they form a cross in
the middle. Fill a jam-jar with water and balance
the potato across the neck of the jar so that the
lower half remains in the water. Keep in the dark
and when the shoots have grown from the eyes,
after about a week, cut the potato into sections,
each with its own shoot. Plant each one in a pot,

covered with compost. Grow avocado plants in the same way (except that when the roots begin to grow you transfer the whole pip to a pot leaving the top sticking out). Have patience, they take a long time.

One or two giant sunflowers growing in your garden will fascinate children. They are a vegetable, although you'll probably find them in the flower seed rack in most shops. They are easy to grow and quite hardy. Plant the seeds ½" deep, and 1' apart, in moist and fairly rich soil. They can be grown as a fence or border display since they will reach a height of anything up to 12', or plant them one month before your beans and the latter can climb up their stalks. When the flowers dry out cut the heads off and rub the seeds into a basket, shell them and eat. Or grind the shelled seeds up into sunflower meal which can be used for baked dishes, breakfast cereals, or with fresh fruit rather like wheat germ. Or feed the seeds to your pet birds.

Peanuts grow best in a greenhouse, but if the summer is warm and you can find a sheltered, south-facing spot on a balcony or patio, you can try growing them from a big flower pot. The plant grows from seed and looks like clover, the flowers produce a runner that buries itself in the soil and the peanuts form in masses underground. Pull up the whole root after the plant dies in the autumn, dry the peanuts and eat them. Or roast them in their shells for 20 minutes in a medium oven (300° F), let them cool, shell them and grind them with peanut oil in a blender to make peanut butter. Use about one tablespoon of oil to one cup of peanuts.

Finally, for Hallowe'en, and Jack O' Lantern time, you could raise one giant pumpkin. But be warned — they need a lot of space, about 10' diameter, but they will grow in partial shade. Choose one of the giant varieties, like Big Max, and raise the seeds two or three to a 3" peat pot indoors (or under glass in mid spring). Harden off and plant out in the late spring. Limit the number of fruits that grow on the vine to one,

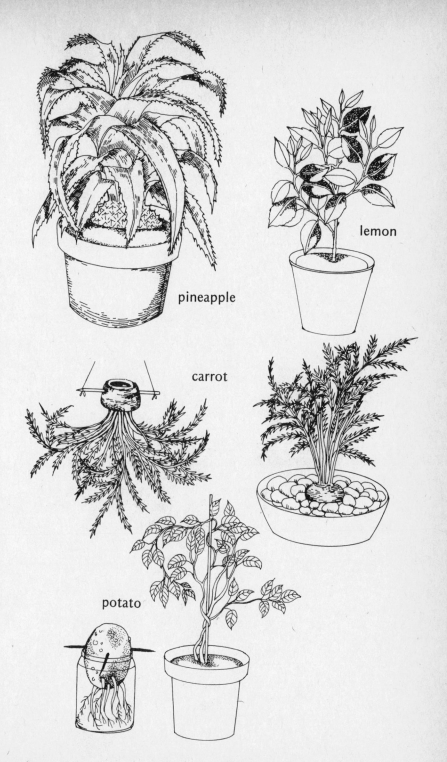

pineapple

lemon

carrot

potato

near the main stem, and remove all others as they appear. Remove most of the foliage and move the pumpkin around as it grows to improve its colour and shape. The pumpkin belongs to the same family as the marrow or melon and the same growing rules apply. By early autumn the pumpkin should be ripe. Stop watering and feeding (just give an occasional watering) and leave it where it is until Halloween. But you must harvest it should the weather be rainy.

PUMPKIN PIE *You need for 5–6 servings:*

*½ pint of pumpkin, peeled, de-seeded, sliced and
    boiled in slightly salted water until tender;
    then sieved
¼ tsp. ground ginger
¼ tsp. nutmeg
pinch of cinnamon
3 eggs
2 tbsp. brandy
¼ pint of milk
4 oz. caster sugar*

Make a shortcrust pastry using about 8 oz. flour. Put pumpkin into a bowl and stir in spices, well beaten eggs, brandy and enough milk to give a thickish consistency. Add sugar and pour into pastry-lined pie-dish. Add top and back in a fairly hot oven for 45 minutes.

HOW TO GROW INDIVIDUAL VEGETABLES

ARTICHOKES, GLOBE

A fine-looking plant to grow in your garden, but
you will need a big one as they are space-eaters.
Globe artichokes are perennial, coming up year
after year, and can be grown in a permanent
plot, except where winters are very cold. The site
should be sunny and sheltered, and the soil fairly
rich and composted.

Sow globe artichoke seeds under glass in early spring, or out of doors a little later. Better still, plant already growing 'offsets' from a nurseryman, about 3' apart and 3' between rows. Water well and feed with a general fertilizer. Watch out for slugs and aphids.

Wait until the second year before you harvest the globes. Cut them off the stalks with a knife, before they open, in the early summer. You should get about fifteen per plant.

In the winter, cut back the foliage and use it as a mulch placed loosely round the plant to protect it from the cold. Or use peat. In the fourth year of growth you should replace the plants by cutting and planting 'suckers', the side shoots.

If you pick globe artichokes when they are really small they can be eaten almost entirely. Otherwise you eat the white, meaty base of the scales or leaves, and the heart. Wash the globes, remove some of the tough outer leaves, and boil them for about half an hour in salted water. When they are tender take them out and turn them upside down to drain. Dip them in melted butter, a vinaigrette sauce, or a lemon, butter and herb mixture. Scrape off the fuzzy, spikey bits before eating the heart.

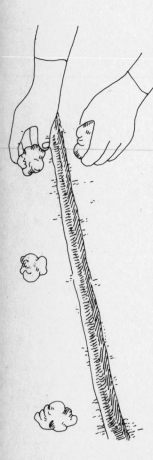

ARTICHOKES, JERUSALEM

Unlike globes, Jerusalem artichokes are grown for their knobbly roots and make a suitable alternative to maincrop potatoes. They are hardy, easy to grow, but also take up a lot of space. They will grow in most kinds of soil, but compost it before planting the tubers.

Make a 4'' to 6'' deep drill and plant the tubers 1½' apart, leaving 3' between drills. Plant in early spring and the crop will be ready for harvesting in the autumn. You should ridge them like potatoes. You can position the Jerusalem artichokes so that their tall foliage, which should be supported, can be used to screen more tender vegetables, like outdoor tomatoes. Watch out for slugs and snails, but little else. Save some of the tubers for replanting the following year.

The knobbly roots can be cooked and eaten just like spuds, except that they are best scrubbed rather than peeled before cooking, and then peeled when served. They can be baked, fried or boiled.

To cook creamed Jerusalem artichokes you should boil them and slice or dice. Make a seasoned white sauce, cheese sauce, or a sour cream sauce (mix it with a pinch of nutmeg and some brown sugar). Heat the artichokes thoroughly in the sauce and then serve. You can cream other rooty vegetables in the same way.

ASPARAGUS

Truly a delicacy among vegetables, but surprisingly easy to grow. You will need to set aside a permanent bed for them, at least 3' square. Asparagus are perennials, so the more early devotion you give them in terms of making their bed a comfortable place to lie, the better they will crop for you.

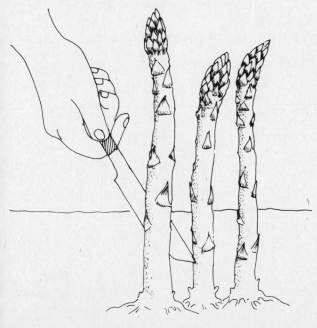

Ideally, make a raised bed from old planks and fill it with a layer of cinders on the bottom, to help the drainage, and then cover with a really weed-free and well composted soil, with some bonemeal added, and lime too if your soil is acidy. A 3' by 3' bed will be able to accommodate two rows of asparagus, planted 18" apart. Buy the young plants, known as 'crowns', from a nurseryman in the spring and put them in the ground as soon as you get them. Buy second or third year old plants ('crowns') because asparagus cannot be harvested till the third or fourth year, and you probably don't want to wait that long. Plant the crowns 3" below the surface and water them well.

Harvest the spears in the summer when they are about 5" or 6" above the ground. Cut the stalks below ground level and stop all harvesting when they start to look thin, as if they've had enough. Keep the bed watered and weeded, and fertilize each spring, and the asparagus will crop for years. Cut back the foliage to just above the ground level in the autumn and put some well rotted compost all over the bed. Watch for slugs, snails, earwigs and the asparagus beetle.

ASPARAGUS A LA BONNE FEMME

8 stems per person
1 oz. butter
2 tbsp. flour
½ pint milk
1 egg

Cut all the stems to the same length and lightly scrape the white part of each with a knife. Lay flat in boiling milk for twenty minutes. Strain off the milk; melt the butter and add the flour and then the milk to get a fine smooth sauce. Then add a lightly beaten egg to make a sauce *à la bonne femme.* Serve with lemon.

Or alternatively, cook the asparagus tied in bundles and standing in boiling water with their tips just above the surface, for about ten minutes. Serve with melted butter and brown bread.

AUBERGINES (egg plant)

Perhaps the most beautiful vegetable of all, oval, shiny, purple, and also good to eat. But the aubergine is not an easy vegetable to grow. It needs lots of warm sun, a sheltered position, and a rich, well drained soil. If your climate falls short of this try growing aubergine indoors, or under glass, in a pot or Grow Bag.

You should at least germinate the plant in this way, unless you buy ready raised ones from a nurseryman. Sow the seeds in early spring in a temperature of at least 60° F, and after germination prick them out and pot singly in

3" peat pots. If it is warm, plant them outside in late spring, when they are about 5" or 6" high, keeping them under cloches if possible. Set them 2' apart, in rows 2' apart, and push a cane into the ground beside them — they will need supporting when they get larger, especially when the fruit forms.

Weed, water and feed with liquid fertilizer. There must not be the slightest check on their growth. Six weeks after planting out you can pinch off the growing tips to encourage the growth of the side shoots, or laterals, which will be the fruit bearers. Syringe the flowers when the weather is dry, to help the flowers set fruit. Once the fruit starts to grow restrict each plant to a maximum of six fruits by removing any extra flowers and stopping the growth of the side shoots. Watch for the red spider mite when the weather is hot and dry, and general wilting.

You can harvest the aubergines from mid summer. Cut them off the plants with a sharp knife before they begin to lose their shine (otherwise they will taste bitter).

Aubergine can be cooked in a number of ways, the simplest being to slice, coat with flour and fried till golden. Or you can parboil, scoop out the middle, stuff and bake them.

ROSEMARY AND EGGPLANT CASSEROLE
that will serve four generously

1 thinly sliced aubergine (big)
2 tomatoes, sliced thinly
1 onion, peeled and chopped
1 tbsp. chopped parsley
4 cloves of chopped garlic
1 dessertspoon of finely chopped fresh rosemary
Salt and pepper
Oil

Place the above in layers in a casserole (do one layer with half and then repeat), put lid on and bake in medium oven (325°F) for one hour.

BEANS

Easy, fast growing and bountiful yielders, with
lots of different varieties, including soya beans
(which contain an incredible amount of protein,
equivalent to four times that of eggs, or twice
that of steak — and many times cheaper). Most
of the varieties also come in two shapes and
sizes, the climbing, or 'pole' beans, and the smaller,
self-supporting, bush varieties. Choose whatever
suits you best.

Climbing beans will climb up poles, walls,
plastic netting, fences or string tied up between
posts, and all without your help. Both climbers
and the bush varieties like to grow in an open,
sunny position, on well composted and well
drained soil.

BEANS, broad (Fava)

Broad beans can be sown directly into the ground
in the early spring in sheltered districts;
earlier if sown under cloches. Or start them
indoors. If your winters are mild you can also
sow in the autumn for an early crop the
following year. Sow the seeds in a flat-bottomed
trench, 2" deep, 9" wide, with 9" between each
seed, in a double row. The growing plants can
share the same central trellis or other support.
Sow a few every two weeks to guarantee a
succession of crops.

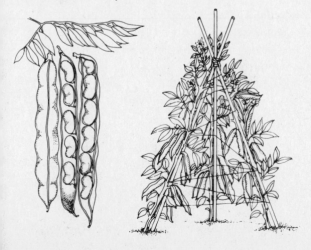

Pinch out the top of the plant when the flowers appear as this will help to discourage blackfly — you must also watch out for mice and the bean beetle. Harvest them throughout the summer, when they are young and tender and at the height of their flavour.

Broad beans can be eaten raw, in a salad, boiled and tossed in butter, with some parsley (if you pick them at their youngest and tenderest you can cook and eat the whole pod with the seeds still inside).

FIST FISTUQIA (a Middle-Eastern dish of beans and yoghurt)

1½ lb. broad beans
1 egg
2 tbsp. rice
yoghurt
salt and pepper
1 clove of garlic

Boil the beans for twenty or thirty minutes, and the rice. Drain both and mix them together. Stir the crushed garlic into the yoghurt, add to beans then the rice and season. Heat and add the beaten egg, stir and serve when it thickens.

BEANS, dwarf French (Kidney or Haricot)

These are probably the best bet for the small space farmer since they take up less room than either broad or runner beans, are good croppers, easy to grow, require no support and are very tasty.

They like a well dug soil. Sow the seeds directly in the ground in mid spring, as soon as the soil has warmed up a bit, or earlier under cloches, and sow a few every fortnight till early summer. Sow a double row, 2" deep and 6" apart, leaving a foot between the two bean rows

and 2' between them and the next row. You
should dress the ground with fertilizer about a
week before sowing. You won't have much in
the way of pests and diseases to worry about.

The beans can be harvested from early summer
till the autumn, when the pods are 3" or 4" long,
and still young and tender. When gathered very
young, before the seeds start to swell, they can
be cooked whole as *haricots verts*.

To make a delicious haricot soup you will need:

½ *lb. haricots*
2 *oz. butter*
2 *onions (chopped fine)*
½ *pint milk*
1½ *pints water*
parsley (chopped fine)
salt and pepper

Soak the beans overnight and drain them. Fry in
butter with the onions then add the water till
they are tender. Push the lot through a sieve, add
the milk, parsley, salt and pepper, and re-heat.

BEANS, runner

Runner beans are the most attractive of the bean family, with both red and white flowered varieties, as well as dwarf selections that can be grown in pots. They like a sheltered position, and a rich soil just as the others.

Runner beans are tender to frost so should not be sown in the open till all danger of frost has passed. Best first to raise them indoors, or under glass in peat pots, sowing them in mid spring; plant them out in late spring, or repot. Put one seed in each 3" pot, or sow 2" deep in a double row, 6" apart, with 1' between

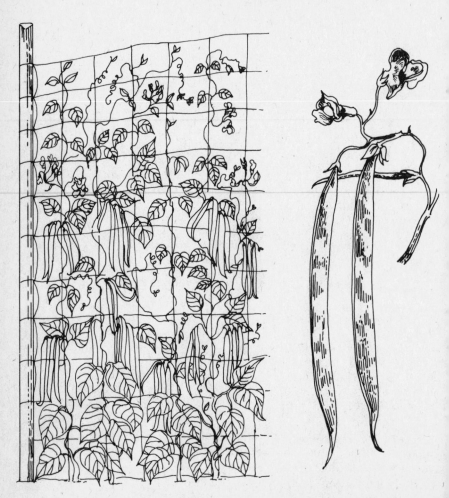

the double row and 2½' between them and the next vegetable. All but the dwarf varieties need to be supported in the way described on p. 85 Thin them to 1' apart as soon as they look overcrowded. Water well, fertilize prior to planting, watch for aphids and slugs, and pinch the growing tips when they reach the top of their pole (except dwarfs).

The runners should be ready for harvesting during the summer and through till the autumn if you plant them as a succession crop. Their yield will be heavy, as much as 40 lb. for a 10' row.

Runner beans can be boiled whole, split, sliced, or chopped and then boiled. The bigger the bean pieces, the longer the boiling time, although always keep it to a minimum. After boiling they can be sautéd in butter and garlic before serving.

BEETROOT

Although beetroot, as its name suggests, is grown primarily for the root, the tops can be eaten too. It is easy to grow but not as nutritious as many other vegetables which will compete for its growing space in a small area. While beetroot prefers a well dug and composted soil, it will grow almost anywhere.

Sow the seeds for a succession crop from mid spring to early summer, or earlier under glass. The drills should be 1" deep and 1' apart. Place three seeds every 6" and later thin to one in each position. Dress with fertilizer before sowing and water and hoe well. Watch out for snails and birds. Harvest your beetroot while they are still small, just larger than a golf ball. They are more tender and tasty then and will probably be ready by mid summer. You should twist off the foliage rather than cut it, otherwise the beet will sadly bleed.

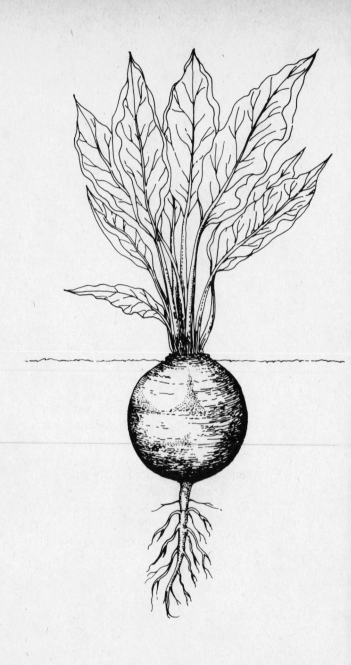

Beetroot can be eaten hot, boiled, steamed or
baked, or cold in a salad. Cook the tops and eat
them like spinach. To make genuine RUSSIAN
BEET BORSCHT you will need:

1 quart stock
1 cup beet juice
1 cup beets, cooked and cubed
juice and rind of 1 lemon
½ tsp. tarragon
1 cup yoghurt
1 tsp. soy flour
3 tbsp. nutritional yeast
½ tsp. salt
1 sprig parsley

Blend all the ingredients together until they are
smooth. Chill or heat. Serve garnished with
minced chives (serves 6).

BROCCOLI

There are two distinct types of broccoli: the
sprouting sort (also known as Calabrese or
Italian) and the heading sort (also known as
cauliflower broccoli). Both are hardy and can be
grown through the winter, especially the purple
sprouting variety, which is the hardiest, and the
easiest to grow, therefore making maximum use
of your space. Broccoli likes cool and moist
conditions, provided the plants never become
waterlogged, and, like all brassicas, likes a non-
acid soil.

Broccoli is generally sown in the early spring,
started off first on a seed-bed, or indoors, and
transplanted (firmly) to well dug soil in the late
spring to early summer. Or you can buy the
plants from a nursery. Outdoor sowing should be
in ½" drills, 9" apart, sowing evenly and then
thinning the seedlings to 6" apart. Plant or
transplant, so that there is 2' between plants
and 2' between rows.

Broccoli suffer from the same ailments as
cabbages (see 'cabbage', page 94). Apply a
general fertilizer once the plants begin to form
well. Harvest can begin in early autumn and
continue through to winter by cutting the
outer leaves as they mature, taking 5" or 6" of
stem with them. You will get about 12 lb. for
every 10'.

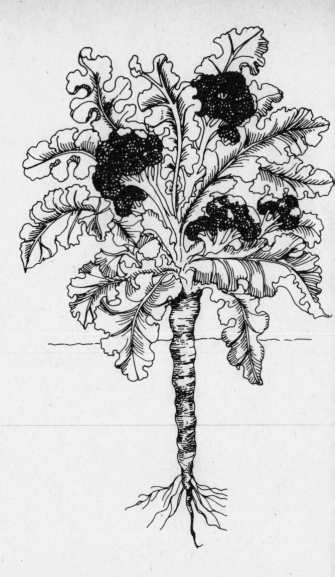

Steam or boil broccoli for about fifteen
minutes. Once it becomes tender drain it carefully and serve with a cheese sauce.

BRUSSELS SPROUTS

Brussels sprouts are like tiny cabbages and
belong to the same family. They are also a cool
weather crop but tend to take up quite a bit of
the urban farmer's likely resources.

Sprouts like a well fertilized and limed soil, previously composted for another vegetable (see the rotation chart). Sow seeds in the seed-bed (if you have one) in early spring, or late winter under glass for an earlier crop. Sow them in ½" drills, 8" apart and transplant firmly whenever they have four or five true leaves, to stand 2' apart with 2½' between rows.

Apply an occasional touch of general fertilizer and keep the sprouts watered. Remove any

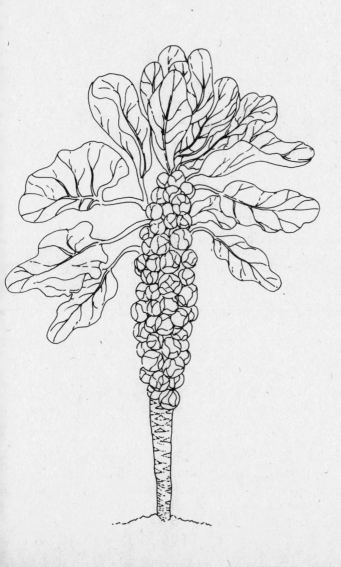

yellow leaves that form, and in early autumn pinch the top of the plant (known as 'cocking') to encourage sprout formation. Harvest them from autumn to spring — their taste is improved by a touch of frost. Gather a few at a time from each plant, starting from the bottom of the stems as soon as the sprouts reach a useable size.

Brussels sprouts are nearly always overcooked. You need only boil them for about 5 minutes, after washing and trimming off their outer leaves. Serve them with blobs of butter.

BRUSSELS SPROUTS SLAW

2 lb. Brussels sprouts
2 eggs
¼ pint soured cream
2 tbsp. melted butter
3 tbsp. vinegar
salt and pepper

Boil the Brussels sprouts as above and put them in iced water to crisp. Drain and thinly slice them crosswise and put them in the fridge to chill. Beat the eggs, sour cream and butter together in a saucepan and heat up the vinegar in another. Pour the vinegar into the mixture, stirring all the time. Do not boil. Remove from heat, add salt and pepper and chill. When ready to serve pour it over the sprouts, toss lightly and serve.

CABBAGES

Cabbages are hardy, easy to grow, and high in vitamin content. But unfortunately they are not very suitable for small spaces, both because of the size of the vegetable and their long growing season. There are lots of different sorts, like red cabbage (ideal for pickling), Pe Tsai, Chinese cabbage, savoys (mild flavoured) as well as several varieties that can be planted at different times of the year, giving you an all-year-round supply. That's if you're really keen on greens. If you want to grow cabbages pick those that mature in late winter and spring so that they don't compete with other crops.

Cabbages, all of them, like a rich, limed soil, never on the acid side. Sow the seeds first in a seed-bed, indoors, or buy the plants from a nursery all ready to be transplanted. Sow outdoor seeds in ½" drills, 1" apart. Thin them as they start to get crowded and about 1–1½ months later transplant them to rows 2' apart, leaving 2' between each cabbage. For spring harvesting, winter growing, sow a hardy variety in the summer. (For the rest of the year sowing, transplanting and harvesting schedules see the chart on page 22). Pe Tsai is sown in early summer and needs only 1' spacing either side.

Feed, during the growing season (dried blood is best), weed and water well. Watch for lots of pests and diseases, like caterpillars, cabbage root fly, flea beatle, white fly, club root, slugs, pigeons, aphids, and so on. The plants are, in other words, very prone to attack.

Harvest time depends on the type and variety you plant, but is always while the heads are still hard and solid.

Cabbage is usually boiled, but why stop there? It can be eaten raw, especially Pe Tsai, or stir fried (wash and cut across the grain into 1" slices and keep moving in the hot oil with garlic and onion for a few minutes). Add soy sauce if you fancy, plus a teaspoon of cornflour mixed with two teaspoons of water.

SWEET AND SOUR CABBAGE

1 large cabbage, shredded
3 grated onions
4 diced tart apples
juice of 2 lemons
¼ cup sweet cider
3 tbsp. honey
2 tbsp. oil
1 tbsp. caraway seeds
½ cup seedless raisins
pinch of ground allspice

Blend all the ingredients in a saucepan. Cover. Simmer gently for ten minutes and serve. Feeds about six people.

CARROTS

Not a difficult crop to grow if the soil is well worked, and a hardy vegetable that will grow in a cool to cold climate, and one with a high vitamin A content. Choose your variety carefully, because there are all manner of shapes and sizes, as well as earlies, maincrop and lates that can be fitted in to your overall layout. The quick-maturing, early varieties will probably suit you.

Carrots grow best in a light, sandy soil, without fresh manure or stones which make the roots fork or grow crooked. Sow the seeds outdoors in mid spring (later for succession crops), or earlier if you raise them under glass or indoors. Sow the

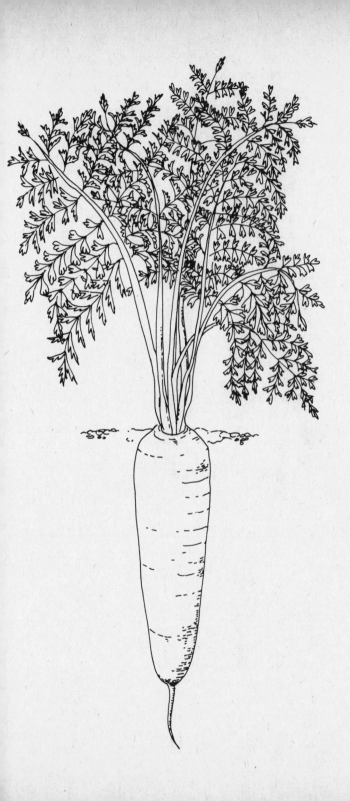

seeds ½" deep in drills 1' apart. Sow evenly and later thin the seedlings to 6" apart, or less if you sow the smaller varieties. Later thinnings are delicious to eat. You should fertilize the soil before sowing, and hoe the ground well while the seedlings grow and after (if you intercrop you will see just where the slow germinating carrots lie). Watch for the carrot fly but little else.

Harvest your carrots from early summer — the yellowing tops will tell you the right moment. Eat them raw, perhaps grated, in salads, with apples, celery or spring onions. Boil or steam them.

SUFFOLK CARROT PIE

6 carrots
6 potatoes
2 separated eggs
salt and pepper
2 tbsp. plain flour

Peel and grate the potatoes. Scrape, wash and dry, and then grate the carrots. Beat egg yolks and add the salt and pepper. Gradually stir in the flour, and when it becomes smooth blend in the carrot and potato. Beat the egg whites till they stiffen and fold into the mixture. Turn on to a greased baking dish and bake in a medium oven (350 degrees) for about forty minutes till golden. Serve it with some cold meats to about four people.

CAULIFLOWER (see also cauliflower broccoli)

Cauliflowers need V.I.P. treatment and should not really be attempted by the freshman urban farmer. If you really like the taste, grow heading broccoli instead because they are less demanding yet similar in flavour.

Like most vegetables, cauliflower likes a sunny but sheltered position, and a well composted, deeply dug and well-drained soil. Outdoors the seeds can be planted in mid spring, after the danger of frost has passed, but you can speed up

your crop by sowing indoors, or under glass in a
frame or greenhouse, a month or two earlier.
You can also use your glass protection for
autumn sowings, ready to be planted out in the
spring. Sow the seeds ½" deep in a seed bed and
transplant to stand 2' between plants.

Cauliflower will benefit from an occasional
general fertlilizer, a regular watering programme
and protection from a strong sun by bending the
leaves over the heads, known as curds. Watch
out for all the same things as you do for

cabbages. Harvest your crop, if you succeed, from mid summer to early winter, before the curds begin to separate into sections. You should get about 10 lb. for a 10' row.

Cauliflower can be cooked whole or broken into sections.

CAULIFLOWER CURRY

2 medium sized cauliflowers
3 tbsp. butter
½ tsp. ginger
½ tsp. salt
½ tsp. turmeric
½ tsp. cayenne pepper
pinch of cinnamon
½ tsp. coriander
½ tsp. mustard seed
½ tsp. cumin seed
1 clove of garlic
¼ pint of water
½ lb. peas
2 diced tomatoes
1 tbsp. chopped parsley

Heat the butter and stir in the spices. Break the cauliflower into small flowers and add them to the pan, then add the water. Cover and steam the cauliflower till tender. Add peas and parsley and cook for another five minutes, stirring all the time. Just before serving add the tomatoes. Serves four hungries.

CELERY (and Celeriac)

Celery takes a lot of time and trouble to grow, but if it appeals grow the easier varieties, the white rather than the red or pink, the self-blanching sort that doesn't need 'trenching', and even choose celeriac, a relative that is grown for its bulbous root rather than the stalks.

Celery likes a very rich soil, well fed, deeply dug and carefully and finely prepared. Prepare a 1' deep and 1½' wide trench. Add a good layer of compost in the bottom and return the soil to bring the level up to 6'', leaving the surplus on

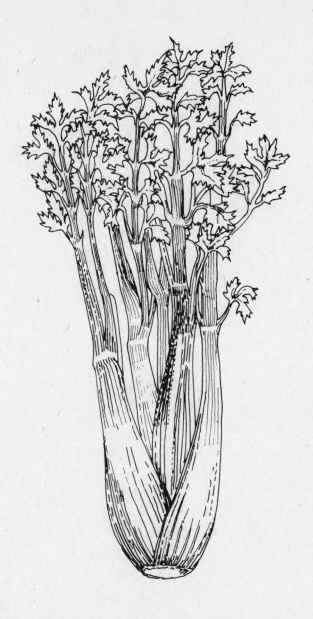

ridges on either side of the trench, and then sprinkle on some general fertilizer.

Sow the seeds in early spring, indoors or under glass, ¼" deep. After about 7 or 8 weeks, when the seedlings are 4" or 5" high, gradually harden them off. Plant the seedlings in the trenches in late spring, 9" apart. The self-blanching varieties can be planted 6" apart in ordinary rows, 1' apart, and the same goes for celeriac. Or you could save yourself this trouble and buy plants from a nursery. Firm the plants well in the ground.

Water, weed and feed the plants well. They are great drinkers and eaters. And watch for the celery fly. Ordinary varieties of celery need to be blanched otherwise they will taste bitter. In early August tie some newspaper loosely round the stems and build up the soil taken from the pile alongside the trench. Do this week by week until only the tops of the leaves can be seen. With celeriac you should draw the soil down from the plant and cut any side shoots that are growing from the roots, a few at a time.

Celery will be ready for harvesting from late summer and on into early winter. Drive a spade into the soil just below the plant to cut the celery at the roots, or lift out celeriac roots with a fork.

To prepare celeriac for eating, scrub the root, top and either cook in boiling water for 5 or 10 minutes, and serve with a cheese or onion sauce, or use it to flavour soups. Or grate it and eat raw in salads. Celery can be braised or steamed (as can celeriac) as well as eaten in its crisp, raw state, simply dipped in salt.

CHARD, SWISS
(also known as Seakale beet or leefy beet)

An ideal crop for the urban farmer. Swiss chard is a member of the beet family but rivals spinach in taste. It is remarkably easy to grow, quick to mature, hardy and with a high yield in relation to the space it occupies. The vegetable can rarely be bought in the shops because it doesn't travel well, and the leaves are best picked singly so that others can take their place.

You can grow Swiss chard from seed, planted ½" deep and thinned to 1' apart (eat the thinnings as greens). Apart from the odd itinerant aphid or two, the plant is likely to remain pest- and disease-free.

Harvest your Swiss chard from mid summer to early winter, a few stems at a time, and when the crop has gone fork over the ground. The small tender leaves can be eaten raw in salads, while the bigger ones can be cooked like spinach. Boil or steam the leaf stalks like asparagus, and eat them in the same way with melted butter or in a cream sauce. A truly two-in-one vegetable.

CHICORY

Another good choice for the urban farmer. Chicory grows best in a well drained soil, manured for a previous crop, and fertilized. Sow the seeds from early to late spring, in ½" drills, 12" apart, and thin the seedlings to 6" apart. You can cook and enjoy those thinnings like greens. Remove the flowering shoots as they appear and hoe the ground well (or you can mulch it with sedge peat around mid summer). Your chicory will be trouble-free as far as pests and diseases are concerned.

And now for the difficult part. In the autumn you can begin to cut the leaves, as they die, to 1" above the crowns and lift the roots carefully with a fork. Cut the roots from the bottom to make them about 8" long and store them upright, in boxes filled with sand, in a cool place. Take out a few every three or four weeks and force them by planting in a box of soil with the crowns at soil level. Cover with another box and keep them in a kitchen cupboard till the chicons appear.

The chicory chicons can be eaten raw in salads, or cooked by boiling or braising. They go well with young dandelion leaves, tossed lightly together with a salad dressing, or with thin slices of orange.

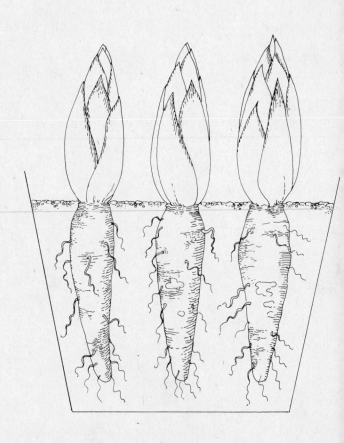

CUCUMBERS

Not really to be recommended for town growing because they take up quite a bit of room, are troublesome to grow, taste no better if eaten freshly picked, are not eaten in great abundance by any one family, have low food value, are always generally available in the shops and are not

particularly resistant to pests and diseases. If that doesn't put you off, here's how to grow them.

There are two main types: ridge for outdoor growing, and frame that need a greenhouse or, as the name suggests, a cold frame. Ridge cucumbers will be your likely choice, and they will need a sunny and sheltered position and a ridge of well-rotted compost mixed with good soil. They are quite happy to be grown in a big pot on a balcony or patio, especially the smaller lemon types, or the Japanese varieties that can be trained up a trellis or wall support.

Sow the seeds indoors or under glass from mid spring in 3" peat pots, 2 seeds to a pot, and let them germinate in a warm place. Thin to the strongest one and plant out in the open ground, or to a bigger pot, in late spring (after first hardening off). If the weather is chilly protect with cloches or jam-jars. Set them about 15" apart. Apart from the varieties that can be grown without any support you must tie the plant to a trellis or cane and train the laterals so that they grow out sideways. Pinch out the growing point of the main stem when it reaches the top of its trellis, or at about 6'.

Water well and give them a weekly feed of liquid manure as the fruits begin to swell. Put some plastic under each fruit if you are growing them 'on the flat' to protect them from possible rot. There is not too much to worry about, but keep an eye out for rots and mildew, plus white fly, aphids and red spider mite. Pick you crop from mid summer to autumn, gathering them small if you want them for pickling (the more you pick the more others are encouraged to grow).

Cucumbers can be fried, stuffed or baked, but are more commonly enjoyed in salads, alongside apple or tomatoes.

ICED CUCUMBER SOUP

2 cucumbers
3 tbsp. cornflour
3 tbsp. milk
butter
salt and pepper
chervil
½ pint of cream

Peel and cut the cucumbers into chunks and boil
them for fifteen to twenty minutes. Drain,
keeping the liquid, and put them through a sieve.
Add the boiling liquid and butter. Heat together
till the mixture starts to simmer. Mix the cornflour
and milk, add it to the soup, and cook for twenty
minutes. Let it cool, adding chervil, salt, pepper
and half a pint of cream and chill it before serving.

FENNEL (Finnochio)

The same family as celery, but grown for its
aniseed tasting roots, and also for its fine looking,
foliage. And it is easy to grow.

Sow the seeds in ½" drills, 1½' apart, and thin
the seedlings to 8" apart. Sowing can begin in
the spring and carry on through to mid summer
for a complete succession programme. You
should earth up the lowest leaf stalks about a
month before using the roots, to help blanching.
Harvest about three months after sowing, when
the roots are the size of tennis balls.

Before cooking, remove the bottom part of
the stem and the coarse outer leaves. Boil in
salt water till they are tender, about ten minutes,
or add to soups for a subtle flavouring. The
innermost hearts can be eaten raw, grated or
sliced into salads.

To make *fennel à la niçoise,* you will need:

2 or 3 roots
2 onions
2 cloves of garlic
4 tbsp. oil
4 or 5 tomatoes

¼ pint white wine
pinch thyme
salt and pepper

After boiling the roots, drain them and quarter.
Chop and sauté the onions with crushed garlic in
the oil till soft. Add the fennel. Peel and chop up
the tomatoes and add these. After a few minutes
add the wine, thyme and salt and pepper. Cover
and gently simmer for half an hour.

KALE

Green or purple, curly or variegated, kale is a beautiful looking vegetable which is easily grown. It is hardy, with a high vitamin content, and an ideal substitute for broccoli. Kale can be grown in tubs, or in the open ground in rich, well-drained soil.

Sow the seeds in mid spring in drills ½" deep, 20" between rows, and thin the plants to 20". Kale is grown in a similar way to cabbage and will benefit from an occasional feeding with liquid fertilizer. Watch out for the same pests and diseases as cabbage, but kale is much more resistant.

Harvest kale from late summer onwards, either taking the leaves from the bottom, as you want them — and more will grow in their place — or cutting whole.

The inside leaves can be eaten raw in salads or sandwiches, and the outer leaves can be prepared and cooked in the same way as spinach.

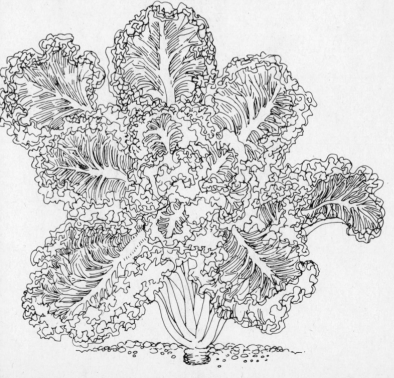

KOHL-RABI

An unusual-looking vegetable that is rarely found
in the shops, and therefore a worthwhile choice
for the urban farmer. It is a hardy plant, a
member of the brassica family, that is grown for
its swollen turnip-shaped stem which develops
above the ground. The roots and the leaves are
of no use and should be composted.

Sow kohl-rabi in a well composted soil from
mid spring till mid summer as a succession crop.
Sow in drills ½" deep 15" between the rows

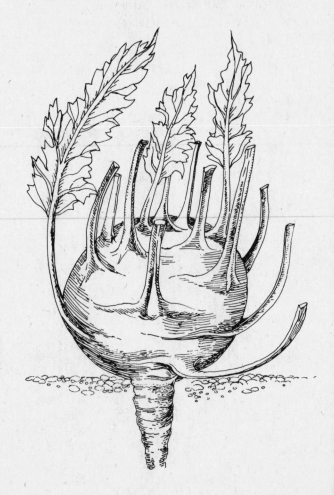

and thin the plants to 6" apart. Water the plants well to keep them growing quickly and watch for aphids, but rarely other problems. Harvest from early summer to early winter when the stem has swollen to the size of a tennis ball.

Kohl-rabi can be eaten raw or cooked, after first peeling and slicing thinly; when cooked it has a sort of turnip/cabbage flavour.

To make kohl-rabi with noodles you will need:

3 oz. butter
2 finely chopped onions
6 kohl-rabi, peeled and sliced thinly
2 tbsp. flour
1 beef stock cube
a carton of sour cream
3 tbsp. chopped parsley
1 tbsp. chopped dill
pinch of thyme
salt and pepper
½ lb. noodles

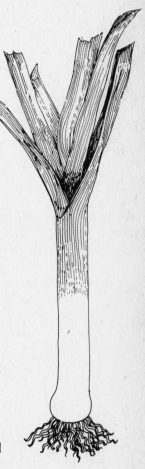

Cook the noodles. Sauté the onions and the kohl-rabi in butter, stirring all the time. Add the flour and cook until lightly browned. Dissolve the stock cube in ½ pint of hot water, stir till boiling and keep boiling for 2 minutes. Add the herbs and seasoning, cover and simmer for 20 minutes. Add the noodles and cream. Cook for another five minutes and serve.

LEEKS

Leeks are mild-flavoured members of the onion family, and hardy. They should be grown in a very rich, well composted soil.

If you grow leeks from seed, first dig a trench 6" deep, add fertilizer, and sow the seed along the bottom ¼" deep. Thin them to 6" apart as the seedlings begin to grow, and when they are 7" or 8" tall you should slowly fill up the trench around the stems to blanch them. Alternatively you can raise seedlings in a seed-bed or indoors and transplant them, or nursery plants if you prefer, to 6" deep holes made with a dibber. Do this in late spring. If you have more

than one row they should be 1' apart. Simply drop the plants in the hole so that only the tips of the leaves are above the soil level, and fill the holes up with water, not soil.

Leeks are rarely troubled provided you water them well during their steady growing period, and perhaps give them a feed of liquid fertilizer in the summer. They should be ready for harvesting from early autumn onwards.

Leeks can be boiled, braised until tender, used for flavouring soups and stews or served *au gratin:*

POTATO AND LEEK PIE

6 big leeks
6 potatoes
2 oz. butter
1 oz. plain flour
1 pint of milk
2 oz. grated cheese
salt and pepper

Grease a baking dish and line the bottom with potato slices and leeks cut to 1". Melt the butter, stir in the flour, and when frothy add the milk and continue stirring till it boils. Add salt and pepper and pour over the vegetables. Cover and bake in a moderate oven (350 degrees) for ½ hour. Then remove the lid, cover the surface with wheat flakes and a few dobs of butter, and put back into the oven without the lid for another ten or fifteen minutes. Enough for four people.

LETTUCES (and endive)

An absolute must in every food grower's plans. They are small, easy to grow, quick maturing and come in all sorts of varieties to suit everyone's requirements.

There are three main types of lettuce, in addition to endive: cos (or 'romaine'), cabbage (or 'head') and leaf. Grow some of each. They all like a rich soil, manured for a previous crop and limed if at all acidy. They prefer the sun, except during hot summer months, and benefit from a general fertilizer before being sown. But you will probably end up growing them all over the place, fitting them in odd corners whenever you get a bit of free space.

Sow the seeds indoors or under glass in winter, under cloches in early spring, or directly in the open from mid spring onwards. Sow a few every fortnight until late August for a continuous supply during your salad days. Some hardy varieties can be sown in the autumn for a spring crop, protected by cloches or grown in frames or indoors. Sow ½" deep and thin to 9" as soon as the true leaves appear (dwarf varieties take up less space than that) or sow pelleted seeds at their proper growing stations. If you grow lettuces in rows they should be 1' apart. Or you can buy seedlings to plant out, although lettuce is one of the least troublesome to grow from seed of all the vegetables.

Water lettuces well, hoe regularly, and feed occasionally; lettuces must be grown as quickly as possible to guarantee their crispness. But do watch out for aphids, fungi, earwigs, cut-worms, leafhoppers, blights and rots, although the seeds you buy will often be resistant to a lot of these. Endive must be blanched to improve its taste — cover it four weeks before picking with an inverted flower pot (with the drainage hole covered too) to cut out the light. Or use cloches covered with black plastic.

Harvest regularly from early summer till the autumn, before they 'bolt' or run to seed. If you don't end up with a glut of bolted lettuces. your careful succession sowing will have been successful. Only leaf lettuce should not be picked whole — just take a few leaves at a time when you want them. And when preparing your salads always tear lettuces by hand, and never cut them, and always wash and dry them well before adding a dressing. Make just a green salad, rather than always serving lettuce with another vegetable. And try braised endive, rolled and stuffed too.

MARROWS AND COURGETTES/ZUCCHINI (summer squash)

There are trailing marrows and bush marrows, both of which yield well, but the bush varieties take up less room and are marginally easier to grow, although trailers can be trained up walls and fences to save space. Courgettes are merely small marrows, picked early, but if you prefer to grow these you should pick a specific courgette variety as they will taste better.

Grow marrows in a heavily composted soil. In mid spring sow the seeds under glass or indoors, putting two to each 3" peat pot, ½" deep, and germinate in the warm. Thin to one and plant out in late spring, allowing 2½' diameter for a bush marrow, and make sure they can get plenty of sun. Towards the end of spring you can sow marrow seeds directly in the open ground, four seeds to a 1" hole. Cover with a flower-pot till germination takes place and then cover with a jam-jar or cloche. Thin to one plant per hole. Or you can buy plants from a nurseryman all ready to set out.

It helps to pollinate the female flowers, those with a swelling behind — the marrow to be — by picking a male flower and inverting it over the female. Take off the petals of the male flower first. Water the marrows well, to reach the roots rather than the leaves and stalks, and feed with a liquid manure when the fruits start to swell. Watch out for aphids, slugs, grey mould, mildew, the cucumber beetle, the U.S. squash bug and caterpillars.

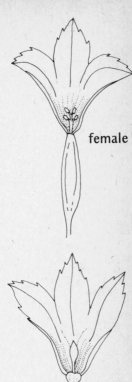

female

male

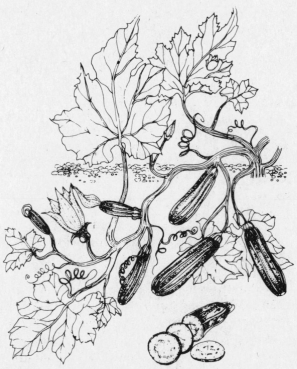

Pick them when you want to from early summer onwards, and the more you pick the more you will get. You can eat the stalks, flowers and leaves, as well as the fruit, for they all combine to make genuine minestrone.

MINESTRONE

2 onions
Flower petals, torn-up leaves and chopped up
    stalks of courgettes
1 lb. tomatoes
2 lb. courgettes
1 pint stock
1 cup mini-pasta

Sauté the chopped up onions, add the petals, torn-up leaves and chopped stalks. Add a pint of stock and simmer for fifteen minutes. Then add finely chopped tomatoes, followed soon after by diced zucchini and finally mini-pasta.

STUFFED MARROW

1 large marrow
6 oz. mince meat
3 oz. cooked rice
1 onion, chopped
3 oz. cooked peas
1 tomato, peeled and chopped
parsley
salt and pepper
1 egg, beaten

Cut the marrow lengthwise and remove the seeds by hollowing out the middle. Mix together the rest of the ingredients and fill the marrow halves and wrap them loosely in foil. Bake in a moderate oven (350 degrees) for forty-five minutes, until the marrow is tender. Serve with a cheese sauce.

One other variety of marrow which should be mentioned, vegetable spaghetti, is grown in the same way. Cook whole for half an hour, cut in half and scoop out the spaghetti-like insides. Serve it with tomato sauce, on April Fool's Day.

ONION SETS, AND SHALLOTS

Don't bother to grow onions from seed, except for spring onions, which are well suited to a window-box, and 'here-and-there' growing. 'Sets' are far easier to grow and are really small bulbs.

Prepare your soil well, carefully removing all weeds and stones, but do make it firm and finely raked. You should add lime, in the winter, if your soil is acidy. Plant the sets in early spring, leaving just the tip of the neck above the surface. Place them 6" apart, in rows 1' apart, and firm the soil round them. Weed well, using a hand trowel to avoid risk of damaging the roots, and water well whenever the soil becomes dry.

Shallots, which have a slightly milder flavour than onions, and are hardier, can be planted from the end of winter. One shallot will produce several shallots, but one onion set will produce only one onion. So plant them a little wider apart, 9".

Watch for eelworms, onion fly, white rot, and thrips, but onion sets are less prone than seed onions, and shallots less prone than onion sets.

By mid summer your crop should be ready (shallots a month earlier) — the tops start to yellow and bend over, just before the flowers starts to form. Leave the onions in the ground for a week or so for a final ripening off, lift them with a fork and lay them in the sun to dry. Or put them in a cold frame. You can boil, bake, fry or eat onions raw, although the latter should be done in moderation. (Shallots are the best for pickling.) Or make an onion tart.

ONION SOUP

5 oz. butter
4 onions, sliced
3 tbsp. flour
¾ pint of water
pinch of thyme
1½ pints potato-peel broth
2 tsp. lemon juice
salt and pepper
sliced French bread
grated gruyère

Sauté the onions in the butter. Add water, broth, flour, herbs, salt and pepper and lemon juice. Simmer for an hour. Pour into a casserole with

bread and sprinkle cheese on top. Bake in a hot
oven for fifteen minutes. Serve six people
immediately.

PARSNIPS

Not really a wise choice for the town. They are hardy (the taste is actually improved by frost) and straightforward to grow, but will occupy the ground for a long time. Parsnips like deeply dug soil and cannot be grown on any small-pot or tub scale. A lot of people don't like parsnips very much either.

However, if you do want to press on, start by breaking down any remaining lumps in your soil and removing large stones that will block the growing root, causing it to fork. Sow the seeds in spring (and, if mild, also perhaps in the autumn, ready for the spring) in drills 1" deep and 15" apart. Place three or four seeds at a time 8" apart and thin to one, or use pelleted seeds. It is a good idea to sow radishes in the same place at the same time. You will harvest them long before the parsnips will need the space, and the radishes will show you just where you shouldn't hoe. Your parsnips may get a dose of canker, but nothing else.

Dig out the roots, when you need them, from early autumn onwards, leaving what you don't need in the ground, all winter if you like. Boil, fry or bake them or turn them into wine. Prepare by peeling and cutting away the hard core.

PARSNIP CROQUETTES

3 or 4 parsnips
2 oz. butter
½ cup milk
1 egg
1 cup of grated cheese
breadcrumbs

Boil parsnips and drain. Mash them with butter and milk and dry off the liquid over a low heat. Beat the egg into the mixture and the grated cheese. Shape and coat with breadcrumbs and deep fry. Beware of the parsnip's reputed aphrodisiac qualities. Or, rather, enjoy them.

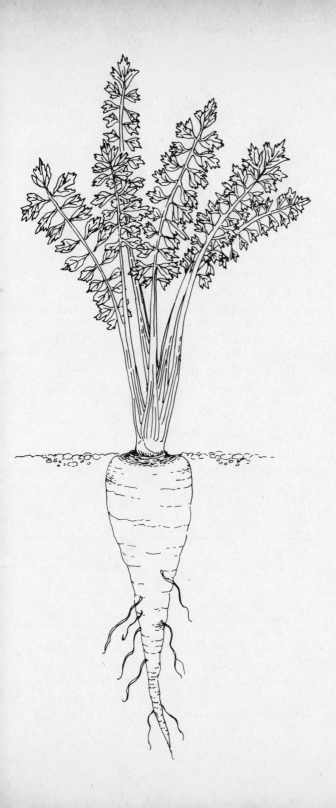

PEAS

Peas are not all that easy to grow but no vegetable-raiser worth his salt could really turn them down. They are highly nutritious and when cooked fresh from the ground, before their sugar content has turned to starch, their sweet, milky flavour is one of the finest you'll experience. Look carefully through the seed catalogues, for there are scores of varieties to choose from, including *mangetout* (with edible pods — also called sugar pea) and petit pois.

Peas are deep rooted vegetables, so like a deeply dug, composted, non-acidy soil, finely tilthed, fertilized and firmed before planting. There are two categories of seed, the early 'round seeded' which are the hardiest and therefore the first batch to be planted, and the 'wrinkle seeded' which follow and are tastier. Sow the round-seeded indoors or under glass in late winter, outdoors in early spring and in the autumn with cloche protection. Sow the wrinkled variety in late spring, in succession (always sow little and often). Never plant out in the cold and wet because the seeds will rot; use cloches to warm up the soil.

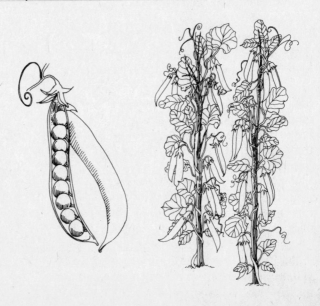

For outdoor sowings make flat-bottomed trenches, 6" wide, 2" deep, using a spade. They should be 2' from the next row. Place two rows of seed in each trench, alternating from side to side, 3" to 4" apart. Place a central support of wire netting, bamboo poles or brushwood in the trench and return the soil, firming it down well. Only dwarf varieties can be grown without the support, and may be most suitable for a small garden, or tub and patio culture. But don't forget that a south-facing wall or fence can also be adapted to any climbing plant.

Weed often, by hand if you plant in a double row, and keep a look out for aphids, the pea moth (or rather its maggots), pea weevil, mice, and protect seeds and seedlings against the birds.

Pick as your pods fill, from early summer onwards till autumn, and from the bottom upwards, and only when you are ready to eat them. Pick *mangetout* before the pods begin to bulge with their seeds. When all the peas have been harvested leave the plants and later dig the roots into the soil.

Use the pods as a base for soups. Everyone knows how to cook peas.

PEPPERS, HOT AND SWEET (capsicums)

Both hot and sweet peppers are grown in the same way as aubergines. There are many types to choose from, such as chili, cayenne, pimento, Spanish, green, and so on, and if you are prepared to give them the growing care they require, they will certainly look impressive as they ripen first to yellow, then to green and finally red.

Peppers are a warm-climate vegetable. They cannot be grown outdoors in cool climates without the protection of glass. This is especially true when raising peppers from seed, a tricky operation that is perhaps best left to a professional and a heated greenhouse. If you want to try, wait till mid-spring and sow the seeds indoors, allow them to germinate in a warm, dark place

and then transfer the seedlings to the sunniest
window-sill. Carefully transplant the seedlings to
3" peat pots, and then to 6" pots as they outgrow
the former. Support the growing plant with a
stake. Don't take them outside till early summer.

Pinch out the growing point when the peppers
show signs of fruiting, and as the fruits swell
water well and feed with liquid fertilizer. Watch
out for red spider mites, and greenfly, but the
chances are your peppers will not be bothered.
Start to harvest in mid summer, as soon as they
are big enough, as picking will encourage more to
come.

Sweet peppers can be eaten raw, in salads, fried, baked and curried.

STUFFED PEPPERS

1 pepper per person
2 onions, chopped
¼ cup olive oil
1½ cups cooked rice
2 tbsp. minced parsley
2 tbsp. raisins
2¼ cups freshly sieved tomato juice
grated cheese

Blanch the peppers in boiling water, removing the stalk and seeds inside. Slice a bit off the bottom so that they can stand upright. Fry the onions and when they become soft add the rice, stir it around, and add the other ingredients except 1 cup of tomato juice and the cheese. Cover and cook till all the liquid has been absorbed. Stuff the peppers and brush the outsides with olive oil. Put them upright in an oiled casserole with cheese on top, and pour the rest of the tomato juice around them. Bake in a medium oven for an hour.

POTATOES

Forget about growing maincrop potatoes. They take up an enormous amount of room, are cheap and abundant in the shops, are rather disease-prone and need quite a bit of work during the growing season. But do consider growing a few earlies as they taste good cooked straight from the ground.

Spuds like a rich, deeply dug and composted soil — they are the only root crop that can be grown on freshly manured ground. You grow them from seed potatoes which you buy early from a reliable source, making sure that they are certified as disease-free. In late winter stand them upright in trays or big pots, with their eye-ends uppermost, and place them in the light indoors to sprout. Remove all but the strongest looking 3

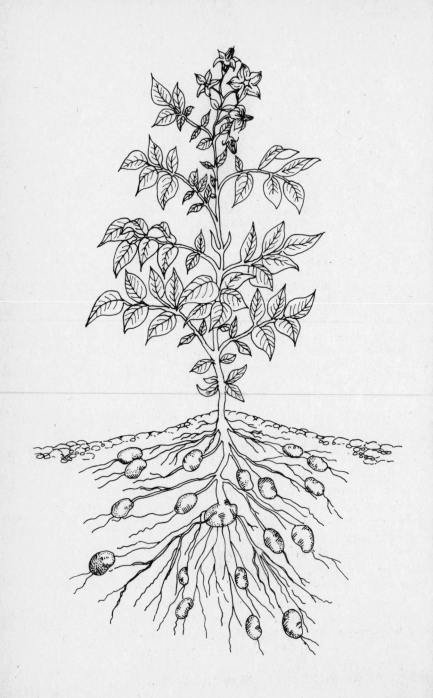

or 4 sprouts (or cut the potatoes into 4 or 5 pieces, each one with at least one strong eye). Start planting in early spring, in a 6" V-shaped trench, or making holes that deep with a dibber. The rows should be 2' apart and the potatoes should be placed, sprouts pointing upwards, 1' apart and covered. Sprinkle the soil with a little fertilizer before sowing.

Hoe frequently between the rows and earth up the potatoes in ridges as they grow, pulling the soil up each side of the plant to make sure that the potatoes have plenty of earth room to develop, and do not come out of the soil.

Watch for eelworms, slugs, wireworms, potato blight, scab, wort disease, the flea beetle, and so on, but don't let all these deter you.

Start lifting the potatoes from early summer, after they've flowered, using the fork carefully so that you do not damage them. New potatoes are best boiled and eaten with their skins, so just scrub them before cooking. Dish them up with lots of butter and perhaps some mint or parsley. To make potato salad, boil the potatoes in salted water but do not let them go soft. Chop up some chives, parsley, 2 hard-boiled eggs and garlic. Mix them with the potatoes as soon as they cool and add lots of mayonnaise.

RADISHES

The easiest vegetables of all to grow, and fast movers. Radishes take up the minimum of room and should be grown in and around all your other crops. They also make a useful marker when planted with slower growers like celery or parsnips. They are not particularly fussy about the soil they live in, as long as it is well tilthed, and don't mind being shaded by taller plants.

Sow seeds under glass or indoors in winter, or outdoors from early spring. Get into the habit of sowing a few every couple of weeks so that you will have a succession of fresh radishes springing up throughout the summer.

Sow seeds ¼" deep; if you sow in rows they

should be 6" apart. Thin the seedlings to 6" apart,
or a wee bit less. Hoe and water to keep them
coming. Watch out for the flea beetle, maggots
and peckish birds, but they will probably stay
healthy.

Start reaping from mid spring right on through
till autumn, or even later if you sow a winter
variety. Eat radishes hot or cold. Cook them
whole, with or without their tops, in a small
amount of boiling water till they are tender
(about 10 minutes). Serve with butter and sea
salt.

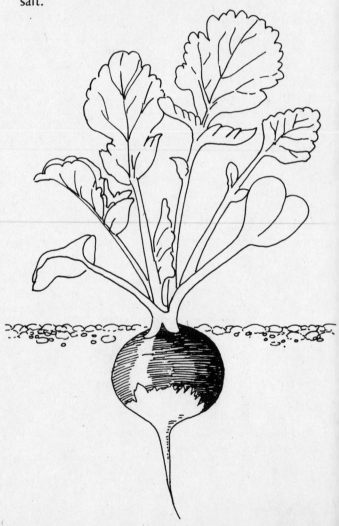

SALSIFY (and scorzonera)

An under-rated vegetable that is known, because of its peculiar taste, as the vegetable oyster. Scorzonera is very similar, grown in an identical way, but with black-skinned roots. Both are hardy and nutritious, but they do occupy the ground for a long time.

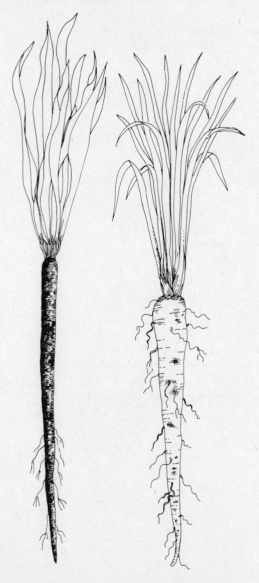

They are cultivated in the same way as parsnips. Make two sowings, the first in early spring and the second a month later, in ½" drills, 15" apart, and thin the seedlings to 9" apart. You should dress the ground with a general fertilizer before sowing. Pests and diseases will not bother salsify or scorzonera.

Harvest begins in the autumn, but, like parsnips, salsify can be left in the ground all winter and dug out in the spring.

Scrub rather than scrape or peel the roots before cooking.

Here's how to make a rather special salsify or scorzonera casserole, using:

8 roots
a chopped onion
juice of half a lemon
1 oz. butter
4 mushrooms, finely sliced
½ oz. flour
grated Parmesan (or other cheese)
salt and pepper
1 tsp. tomato puree
½ cup white wine
½ pint white stock
2 tomatoes
chopped parsley

Cook the salsify in boiling water till tender. Heat the butter in a casserole, add onion and mushrooms, and sauté. Remove from heat, stir in flour, salt and pepper and tomato purée. Return to heat, add wine and stock, and stir until boiling. Simmer for 15 minutes. Cut salsify into pieces, and peeled tomatoes, and put them in. Cook for another 10 minutes, sprinkle on the grated cheese and parsley.

SPINACH

A nutritious and useful crop for the small space grower because it is very quick growing, hardy, and can be conveniently fitted in to your overall plans. Pick the right sort of variety for your climate (New Zealand spinach for example looks different, but tastes the same and is better suited to warm climates).

Spinach grows best in a good, rich soil, well drained and worked fine. Winter spinach must have a sheltered spot. The summer, round seeded, varieties should be sown every two weeks, in small amounts, from early spring to early summer. The winter, prickly seeded, varieties, are sown from August to September, protected by cloches if cold. Sow the seeds 1" deep in drills 1' apart and thin the seedlings to 6". These thinnings can be eaten in salad.

Water well and don't worry about pests or diseases. Buy varieties resistant to blight; apart from that aphids are the only potential threat.

Harvest the summer spinaches from late spring to autumn and the winter ones from autumn to early spring. Pick the leaves continuously from the outside as soon as they are large enough because further leaves will follow.

Spinach is best steamed until it begins to wilt.

KOREAN SPINACH

2 lb. spinach
¾ cup oil
juice of 1 lemon
1 onion, grated
½ cup roasted sesame seeds

Steam the spinach and mix it with the remaining ingredients.

SWEDES (Swedish turnip/rutabaga)

Swedes prefer to grow in a big field. Don't bother with them in town, especially if you decide to grow turnips, which are almost the same but a bit smaller. Just for the record, swedes are best sown in the open in mid spring in ½" drills, 15" apart, and the seedlings thinned to 8". They can be lifted, as required, from autumn onwards. Hoe and water well.

SWEET CORN

Really a cereal, a type of maize, but sweet corn is usually regarded as a vegetable. It takes up a lot of room but is so excellent to eat when cooked fresh that you should try and squeeze it in somewhere. It cannot be grown if your summer is too cold and sun starved.

Sow the seeds in mid spring, indoors, in 3" peat pots. Put two or three seeds in each pot and thin to the strongest looking seedling. If your springs are warm you can sow directly in the ground, 1" deep, putting 3 or 4 seeds in each dibber hole every 15". Don't plant just one row, you should plant at least two, 2½' apart or group four or five plants together to assist pollination. Apply some general fertilizer before sowing.

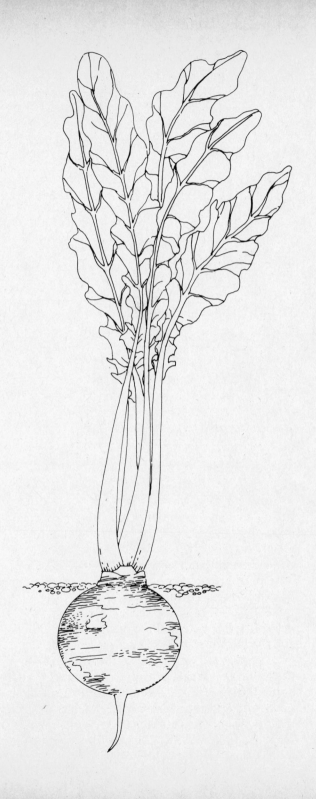

Indoor plants can be transplanted in early summer to their growing positions, after hardening off. Water and weed well. Nothing to worry about except neighbours with long cob-picking arms.

Harvesting will begin around the middle of summer and carry on till early winter. Never pick corn until the pot of salted water is already boiling on the stove. Every second counts in getting the most flavour from your cobs. Ripe cobs will be about 6" long and their tassels will appear droopy and dark. Test them by puncturing with a fingernail; milky juice should ooze out. Always twist them off the stalk.

Popcorn varieties should be left on the plant till the end of the summer. Pick them on a sunny day and leave them to dry. Rub off the cobs and store in the warm for a few weeks.

Remove the husks from sweet corn cobs and boil for a few minutes till tender. Munch off the cob, after coating with melted butter, sea salt and pepper. Or sauté the seeds off the cob. To roast corn place the cobs in a casserole, cover with butter and roast for 30 minutes in a hot oven, turning constantly.

TOMATOES

The life and soul of your urban farm. Look in the seed catalogues to see what varieties will grow in your area and grow several different types, particularly the dwarfs.

Indoors or outdoors, tomatoes need all the sun and warmth they can get. Outdoors they are best grown against a south-facing wall, either from pots or in well composted and drained soil. Since they are very vulnerable to frost, do not attempt to plant them out till all frost danger has passed. Sow the seeds indoors in late winter/ early spring, or under glass outdoors in mid spring, either starting them off in seed-trays or sowing two seeds to each 3" peat pot. Thin to leave the best (or prick off from seed-trays) and harden off towards the end of spring. If you are going to grow the tomatoes from pots you must

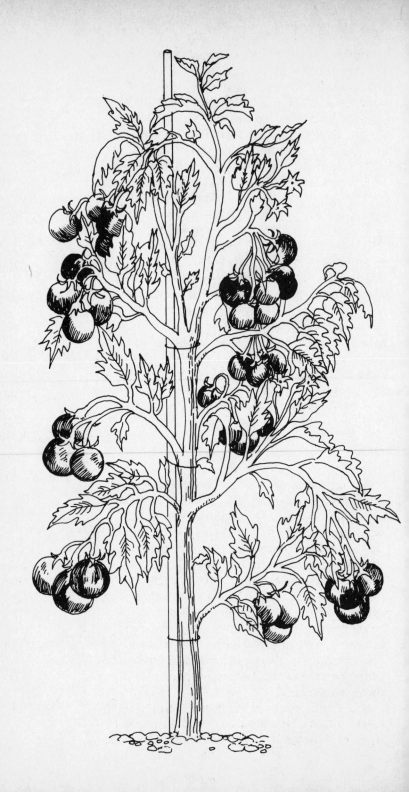

repot the plants to ever larger sizes as the roots fill up their present pots. You should also change the grade of compost, starting off with seed compost, then 'No. 1' potting compost in 3" and 5" pots, ending up with 'No. 3' compost in larger 9" plus pots. Or buy ready-raised seedlings and pot them or plant out in early summer.

Tomatoes planted directly into the ground, when they are at least 6" tall, should stand 1½' apart (and rows should be 2' apart). Water the planting holes well beforehand. Protect them on cold nights with cloches or upturned flower pots. All tomatoes need to be loosely tied, and retied as they grow, to a cane or trellis to support them, except the dwarf varieties. All, again except the dwarf varieties, need to have their side shoots pinched out using your finger and thumb and their growth restricted to a single main stem. This will concentrate the plant's growing energy in one direction. Restrict growth to four or five trusses by pinching out the main growing shoot two leaves beyond the last truss to encourage fruiting, rather than the production of lots of foliage. To assist pollination shake or tap the plants gently when they are in flower, or spray overhead with a water syringe. This will help the fruit to set. Or use a feather.

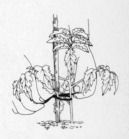

Tomatoes can suffer from several things — stem rot, root rot, blight, leaf mould, mosaic, virus, verticillium wilt, blotches, wire worms, eel worms and red spider mite. The chances of any of these are considerably reduced when tomatoes are grown on a small scale, as opposed to commercially, but to be sure of their immunity you can now buy special tomato sprays that give all-round protection.

Do not overwater tomatoes, especially indoors, but water well and feed with a tomato fertilizer once the fruit begins to set. But don't overdo it or the fruit will split. Hoe regularly if planted in the open ground.

The tomatoes should be ready for picking by early autumn. Pick them as they colour and ripen off indoors in a warm dark place such as the airing cupboard. The earlier you pick the more the plant will bear, up to about 8 pounds a plant if you are lucky. Green ones can be used for chutney. Pull up the old plants when the season finishes and compost.

Tomatoes can be eaten raw, stewed, fried, baked, and so on. They play a crucial role in many dishes.

DEVILLED TOMATOES

1 lb. tomatoes
2 hard-boiled eggs
2 oz. butter
2 pinches of mustard powder
2 tsp. sugar
1 tbsp. vinegar
2 eggs

Slice the tomatoes and put them in a casserole dish, add some blobs of butter and cook for five minutes. In another pan mix together the yolks of the hard-boiled eggs, the butter and the mustard powder, sugar and vinegar. Heat up. Beat two fresh eggs into the mixture and stir until it thickens. Serve the tomatoes on croûtons and cover with the sauce.

TURNIPS

Turnips are hardy and don't like to grow in hot,
dry summers. For a root crop they grow quite
rapidly, and mature one month earlier than
swedes.

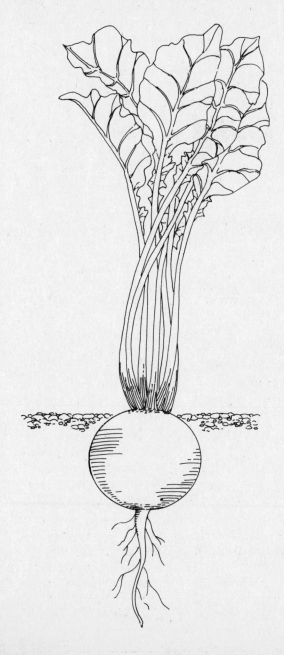

Sow in the open ground successively from early spring to autumn, a small quantity at a time. Earlier sowings must be cloched. Sow in ½" drills, 15" apart, and thin the turnips to 6" apart.

Watch for root maggots, gall weevil, club root, mildew, soft rot, flea beetle (or turnip fly) and aphids. You can begin to lift the roots out of the ground from early summer onwards, whenever they are of a reasonable size.

Boil turnips for about 30 minutes, and then mash or eat whole. The tops contain a lot of vitamins and can be eaten as greens. To bake turnips you should scrub and trim them and cut them into quarters. Sprinkle with some tamari soy sauce and place in an oiled casserole, cover and bake in a moderate oven for just under an hour.

GROWING FRUIT IN TOWN

You probably won't have room for an ordinary fruit tree, let alone a mini-orchard, in your garden or back yard. If you rent your house you may not feel like establishing a fruit tree now for your landlord to begin reaping the benefits long after you've moved on. But you have a host of choices of quick-yielding, space-saving fruit trees and bushes, some of which are even suitable for planting indoors.

APPLES AND OTHER FRUIT TREES

Ordinary fruit trees take up a great deal of space, both above and below the ground, need a long time before they start to bear fruit, and often have to be planted with other varieties to ensure that they are pollinated. Forget them. If you like apples, pears and other tree fruits, go and buy a self-fertile dwarf variety from your local nursery and in a couple of years you will be growing fruit, just as big in size as that from an ordinary tree, but yours will only stand about 4' or 5' high. You won't need special cutting/pruning tools or sprayers, and if the fruit falls to the ground when you're not looking, the chances are that it won't get nearly so bruised! The dwarf tree won't live as long, but it will survive for around fifteen years, producing about 20 pounds of fruit each season. There is even one dwarf apple variety that has been developed to produce several different varieties of apple, including cookers, on the one tree.

Dwarf 'bush' type trees can be grown in big pots or tubs, making them ideal for a sunny balcony or patio, and can even grow indoors if there is plenty of sun, such as in a glass extension unit. Alternatively you might find a cordon will suit you better than a free standing bush tree as the cordon can be trained along a wall, a fence, or even as a screen.

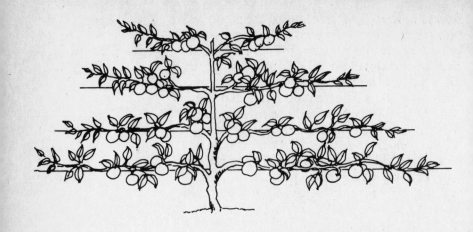

Buy your trees from a nursery or gardening centre. In fact, apart from melons possibly, it's not worth raising any fruit from seed as it is a difficult job. Ask the nurseries' advice about pruning and spraying against pests and diseases. Dwarf trees are already trained when you get them to grow in a certain direction, so you will have to follow these guidelines and try to

maintain the original shape and to let light reach into the middle. Essentially the main branches, or leaders, are cut by half just above a growth bud which points in the direction you want the branch to grow. Side shoots, or laterals, are cut back to one fruit bud. All cuts should be made ¼" above the bud, sloping down away from the bud. You really need a pair of secateurs to do the job properly, and perhaps a specialist book on fruit bush and tree-pruning and training.

Before planting your tree dig the ground thoroughly, way back in the autumn if you can, and add compost. Dig a hole large enough for the roots to spread out. Replace the earth and tramp it down. Cover with a mulch. Pruning takes place in the spring and winter, and all fruit trees benefit from the addition of fertilizer now and then.

Apart from apples and pears, there are tub-size or cordon specimens of most fruits, with varieties to suit your particular climate. Many, like figs for example, are hardier than you might imagine and can be trained against a sunny wall into a fan shape, but they do need a well drained soil (fill the bottom of the planting hole with cinders to make certain).

GRAPES

These can be grown even in a cool and fairly damp English climate provided you give them as much shelter and sun as you can find. They can be grown on balconies, or inside glass-covered verandahs or sun lounges, but buy a variety suitable for the conditions under which you want to grow them.

Plant the vine in the spring and as it grows train it into the shape you want. Vines are best grown against a wire trellis fixed to a wall, or between posts. Restrict the vine just to four arms growing from the main trunk and tie them loosely to allow for growth. You will have grapes in three or four years, but bear in mind that this is a difficult plant to grow.

MELONS

The Cantaloupes are the hardiest types of melon to grow but they still need to be housed under glass, in a cold frame, under cloches, or in a greenhouse in a cool climate. If you have a sunny bay window you could also try growing them secured to wires (the same way as growing them in a greenhouse) and using nets to support the fruit when it starts to get big.

Sow the melon seeds in pots indoors in mid spring. Propagate at a temperature of at least

65°F. Move the melons to their growing positions in early summer and plant them 3' apart. Pinch out the growing tips after five leaves have formed, and restrict the side shoots at two leaves or two beyond each fruit. Don't try to grow more than four fruits on each plant — cut off the surplus growth if others appear.

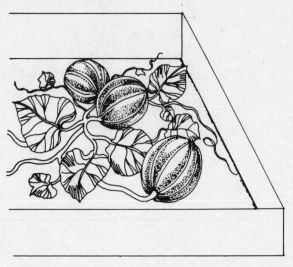

Pollinate the female flowers, those with a tiny fruit forming behind the petal, by using a small, clean paint brush and brushing pollen from male flowers to the centre of the female. Or remember to remove their glass covers on warm sunny days so that the insects can get to work.

Water the melons well as the fruits start to form and give them a taste of liquid fertilizer. Stand the fruits on some pieces of wood to keep

them off the soil (if they lie in water they may rot). Stop watering when they stop swelling. The melons should be ready to eat towards the end of the summer; give the end of the fruit a squeeze with your thumb, just the way to make a greengrocer angry, to test for ripeness.

RHUBARB

Rhubarb is an easily grown perennial plant that needs a complete growing season in the ground before you should start to harvest. Plant the roots, or 'crowns', in early spring in well dug and composted soil, 2" below the surface and 2' apart. Remove flower stalks as soon as they appear. The following spring after your planting year you can lift the stalks from the crowns but never pull too many in one season from one crown. Topdress the soil with general fertilizer and add compost each winter. Be warned, rhubarb leaves are poisonous.

STRAWBERRIES

Alpine and ordinary strawberries are also perennials
that need a year to fruit. Unlike rhubarb, they
can easily be grown indoors, in strawberry pots,
barrels, hanging baskets, and so on. (With barrels
you make 4 rows of 1" holes, 6" apart and
insert the plants as the barrel is filled with
compost.)

Buy and plant plants in mid summer, (15"
apart and 30" between rows if outdoors) with
the 'crowns' just below the surface of the soil or
potting compost. Only Alpines will flourish in
the shade. Remove the blossoms the first year
to prevent fruiting. If outdoors put black plastic
or straw under fruit to keep it off the soil, and
topdress with compost in the autumn. Replace
every three or four years, which you can do
by propagating the 'runners' (the shoots that
creep along the ground and take root) the year
before when the fruit has been harvested.
Indoors they require no special attention.

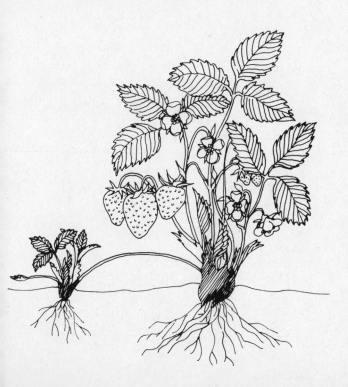

BERRIES, VARIOUS

Berries are easy to grow, take up little space and, if well pruned, will yield well. They can be planted outside, grown from tubs on a balcony or patio (supported by stakes) or trained against walls and fences.

Raspberry canes, or cuttings, should be planted about 2' apart during the late autumn or winter. In the spring cut them down to about one foot. The following autumn cut the fruit-bearing canes to the same level as the ground and shorten the others, those that are to bear fruit the following year, by about a third of their length. Leave just six canes per plant, keeping the centre of the bush open and retaining the strongest-looking ones.

Blackberries are grown in the same sort of way as raspberries except that they should be pruned to leave just the three strongest canes. If you are short of space, forget about blackberries because there will be plenty growing wild in the country-side and the temptation to pick them will get you out of town for a day. If you want a second berry bush, try loganberries, which are grown in the same way, or gooseberries.

Gooseberries should be grown like raspberries but pruned like redcurrants.(see below).

CURRANTS, VARIOUS

Black, white or red, they will yield about ten pounds of fruit per bush, planted 4' apart, or trained against a wall or fence, or in a tub on a balcony. They like sun, but can also thrive in partial shade. Prune blackcurrants like raspberries, but since the fruit of the red and white currants grows on 'old' wood, pruning can be less drastic and more general, cutting back to about half the length all round. Try to end up with three branches for every year of growth.

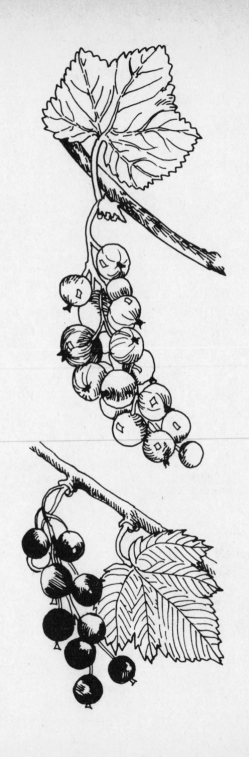

With all currants and berries watch out for greedy birds and net your plants if they start to threaten, particularly gooseberries.

Eating your fruit harvest

Apart from picking and eating raw fruit, perhaps dipped in a little sugar and cream, you can prepare it in any number of different ways. Try tarts, trifles, pies, crumbles, flans, fools, mousse, stewed or souffléd (as the recipe below suggests). Then there are jams to be made, fruits to be candied, bottled, dried; and wine . . .

Use your fruits with home-made *muesli* for a healthy start to your city day. Make the muesli from oats, wheat germ, grated nuts, dried currants, and then add fresh or dried other fruits and serve it with the top of the milk, condensed milk, yoghurt or cream and a blob of honey.

SOUFFLÉ

1 cup finely chopped or puréed fruit
honey
¼ cup unsweetened fruit juice
4 egg whites
1 pinch of salt
1 tsp. grated orange or lemon rind

Beat the egg whites till stiff with the pinch of salt. Mix the fruit with the honey and fruit juice. Fold the egg whites into the fruit and turn everything into a greased dish. Bake at 375 degrees for thirty minutes until it is all puffed up and brown on top (but don't open the oven door to peek before the cooking time is up or the whole thing will sag).

FRUIT PUDDING

¼ cup rye flour
½ tsp. salt

2½ cups boiling sweet cider
1 cup berries
¼ cup honey
1 tsp. oil
4 tsp. grated lemon and orange rind
pinch of nutmeg

Sift the flour and salt into the boiling cider and simmer, stirring constantly. Add the fruit when the liquid begins to thicken and after a minute remove it from the heat and mix in the rest of the ingredients. Eat it hot or chilled.

SOME GENERAL TIPS ON COOKING VEGETABLES

Soggy and overcooked vegetables as an accompaniment to a main meat dish are hardly an appetising thought. But prepared and cooked in the proper way, even the most familiar of vegetables will spark off a revived enthusiasm. Add a few home-grown herbs and the vegetable could well stand in its own right as a main dish. And if the home-grown selections are adventurous, the pleasures of eating your urban farm produce combined with the nutritional content of well cooked vegetables, can easily rival your traditional preference for meat.

To derive both the optimum taste and nutritional value, many vegetables should be gathered when still young and tender and either eaten raw, perhaps in a salad, or cooked as soon as possible. This is not so true with root vegetables, except the early varieties, but with these you should be careful not to over-prepare them for the pot — the best part of a root is near the skin, so young carrots, turnips and potatoes, and so on, should only be scrubbed and older crops peeled as thinly as possible.

The general rule for cooking vegetables is to do so for the absolute minimum time, in the least amount of water if you are boiling them and avoid soaking them when you wash beforehand.

Steaming in a steaming basket is an excellent
way to retain their flavour. Others can be sautéd,
fried, pressure cooked, oven baked, or roasted;
the recipes that are included with the vegetables
described in the book will show some of the
possibilities. To prepare your vegetables for
oriental dishes, chop them up very small and
sauté in a heavy skillet with very little oil. Reduce
the heat, cover and simmer briefly. To 'tempura'
vegetables, dip them in a thin batter and deep-fry.

Here are a few general ideas that combine
several different vegetables:

VEGETABLE CASSEROLE — there are many other variations on this theme — :

1 cup grated beetroot
1 cup chopped celery
1 cup grated turnips
1 cup grated carrots
1 cup sliced onions
½ cup stock
3 tbsp. chopped parsley
1 tsp. chervil

Arrange vegetables in layers in a greased casserole.
Blend the stock and herbs and pour over the
vegetables. Cover. Bake at 350° F for 40 minutes.
Serves 6.

RATATOUILLE

1 onion
1 small aubergine
2 green peppers
2 courgettes
1 small cucumber
2 cloves garlic
1 small chili pepper
4 tbsp. olive oil
½ pint vegetable broth
¼ pint potato peel broth (see over)
small tin tomato purée
2 tomatoes
6 tbsp. vinaigrette sauce (see over)

Chop or slice all the vegetables (the chili pepper and garlic very finely). Heat oil in the pan and start frying the garlic and chili, followed by the onion, then courgettes, aubergines and peppers. Stir well. Mix the broths and tomato paste in a bowl and pour over the vegetables. Add cucumber. Cook slowly till the sauce has gone. After about an hour, when the vegetables should be tender, add tomatoes. Let it cool, add vinaigrette sauce and serve.

VINAIGRETTE SAUCE

3 tbsp. white wine or herb (home-herbed) vinegar
1 tbsp. lemon juice
¼ tsp. mustard powder
6 tbsp. olive oil
salt and pepper

Mix together the vinegar, lemon juice, mustard and salt and pepper. Add the olive oil gradually, stirring fast all the time. Or make the salad dressing in a bowl, first rubbed with garlic. Then add salads and olive oil, toss, then add the rest of the ingredients and toss all together.

Soups and Broths

A blender would be a worthwhile investment, as well as a big pot. The best base for a vegetable soup is vegetable cooking water (you can also reduce it, adding herbs and butter, and use as a sauce over the vegetables) or a broth made from cooked or raw left-overs, and from potato peel. Add other vegetables, herbs, salt and pepper, and perhaps soy sauce, pasta, lentils, barley, and so on. Simmer the lot until the vegetables become soft but add water as it evaporates. For clear soups strain off the liquid. Otherwise force the soup through a sieve, use a mouli or blender. For cream soups add milk or cream and perhaps sour cream just before serving. For a gazpacho, well, why not let your green vegetables determine what goes into it and serve it after chilling well.

A VEGETABLE SOUFFLÉ

3 eggs
cup of thick white sauce
½ tsp. minced onion
½ tsp. mixed herbs
cup of sieved and boiled vegetables
salt and pepper

Separate the eggs and beat the yolks till thick.
Stir into the sauce. Add the onions, herbs and
vegetables, plus plenty of pepper and salt. Beat
egg whites till stiff, fold into the mixture and
turn into a casserole. Bake on middle shelf at
350° F for 35 minutes till puffed up and with a
brown crust. Serves 4.

STORING FRUIT AND VEGETABLES

A small plot of land, a back-garden or yard, or
just a few indoor 'fields', will be sufficient to
provide fresh summer produce. But if you can
manage to grow any surplus crops (or if you
make a mess up of your planning and end up
with too much of one crop) they can be stored
in a variety of ways and provide you with some
supplies for winter consumption. Eat what you
can, and can what you can't. Storing essentially
means no more than preventing decay.

Freezing

A freezer will give you an all-year-round vegetable
plot. Most vegetables can be frozen and will keep
for a year or so without going off, in the same
fresh and nutritious state as when they went in.
It is an ideal way to store beans, asparagus,
aubergine, cauliflower, peas, sprouting broccoli,
spinach, and sweet corn and soft fruits, but not
so good for storing those vegetables that contain
a lot of water and are usually eaten raw, such as
lettuce, tomatoes, celery, cucumber, onions and

radishes and big marrows. Look in your seed catalogues to find out which varieties are best suited to freezing (they are usually indicated).

Freezing is easy. Only use fresh, healthy, unbruised and young and tender fruits and vegetables. This is true for all types of storing. Vegetables have to be blanched in boiling water before freezing and this is best done using a wire basket that will fit inside a saucepan of boiling water. Prepare the vegetables as if for cooking and boil them for the time recommended in your freezer instruction book. Then plunge the basket into cold water, let them cool, drain, dry on absorbent paper, pack into plastic bags, seal the bags, label, date and freeze. Try to exclude as much air as possible before sealing the bags (they must be airtight). When you cook the vegetables there will be no need to thaw them first, with the exception of asparagus and sweet corn. Cook them for half the normal cooking time of the particular vegetable. Never re-freeze, so you should pack only in sufficient quantities for one occasion.

Soft fruits need only to be bagged, sealed and frozen. Blackberries and strawberries should be packed with a sugar syrup made from one cup of sugar to one pint of hot water.

Drying

Some fruits and vegetables can be preserved simply by storing them in boxes in a dark, frost-proof shed, cellar or attic. Root crops, for example, do not need to be eaten fresh like peas, beans or lettuces, except the early, tender varieties of beets, carrots and new potatoes. Some can be left in the ground all winter, like Jerusalem artichokes and parsnips, but you will probably want to use the space for other things. Put the roots in boxes of sand or peat and arrange them in layers so that no two vegetables are touching each other. Apples can also be stored in the same way. The sand or peat keeps the air out, the temperature constant and absorbs moisture.

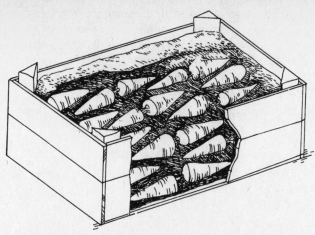

Other fruits and vegetables are best dried out if you want to preserve them. Onions and herbs can be tied and hung in bunches. Onions should be first dried by bending over their tops when they are ripe and then lifting them out of the earth and laying them out in the sun, occasionally turning them, for about ten days. Or use a cold frame if the weather is poor. Herbs should be picked before they flower (after the dew has dried) and hung upside down in bunches (if you dry them outside cover with paper bags to shield them from direct sunlight). Or you can dry them by spreading out on home-made drying trays (see below). They are dry when they crackle when touched. Store in airtight jars.

Apples (also pears, grapes, plums and figs), peas, beans and mushrooms will store well if dried out completely before being packed away in cardboard boxes and kept in a dry place. Make a drying tray from an old picture frame with cheesecloth, muslin or nylon net stretched across and tacked to the sides. Place the prepared fruit or

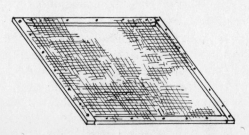

vegetables on the trays and leave to dry under a strong sun, in an airing cupboard, or in front of a fan heater. Vegetables are usually blanched first (the same way as for freezing, usually for about three minutes). You can also dry in an oven using the ordinary shelves, a low heat and leaving the oven door ajar. Apples and mushrooms can be dried by threading them on to a string (peel and slice the apples into rings first, core them, and dip them in some salt water to prevent browning) and hanging them over the stove for a few hours.

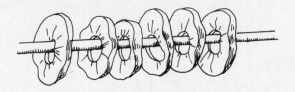

All dried fruits and vegetables can be revived by soaking them in a small amount of water and cooking them in the usual way.

Making jams

Start your jam making by saving plenty of screw-top jars well ahead of the fruiting season. Apart from those you will need a large enamel or aluminium pan and a wooden spoon.

All kinds of fruit, and some vegetables, can be made into jam. Wash the fruit and remove the stems and stones if they are big. Simmer the fruit in water until it becomes soft and a bit mushy. Some fruits (cherries, strawberries, rhubarb, pears, marrows, etc.) will need the addition of a couple of tablespoonfuls of tartaric acid or lemon juice to help the jam set. Add sugar (see below for the amount). When it has dissolved, boil rapidly until the setting point is reached, and stir it now and then. As a test for the setting point put a spoonful on a cold plate, leave it for a couple of minutes, and then the jam should wrinkle when you push it with your finger.

Remove the scum from the surface and pour the jam into all those clean, warm and dry jars, filling them just short of overflowing. Press greaseproof paper evenly over the surface without leaving any gaps or air bubbles. Clean the neck of the jar and put the top on. Wait till tomorrow's breakfast to sample your results, and store the jars in a cool, dry place.

Some jams to try (to make 5 lb. of jam).

BLACKBERRY AND APPLE:

2 lb. of blackberries, ¾ lb. of peeled, cored and sliced apples, 3 lb. of sugar and half a pint of water.

GOOSEBERRY:

Top and tail the gooseberries, 2¼ lb., ¾ pint of water, 3 lb. of sugar.

MARROW GINGER:

4 lb. of peeled, cubed and de-seeded marrow chunks. Steam until tender, put in a basin, cover with sugar and leave overnight. Add 1 oz. of ginger, 4 tbsp. lemon juice, 3 lb. of sugar. Cook in usual way.

Candied fruit

A real sickly treat. Prick small fruits with a fork so that they won't split open when cooking, peel, core and slice others. Cook slowly till tender. Drain. Boil together two cups of water and one of glucose (more if you need it to cover the fruit) and pour it over. The next day pour the syrup off into cups. For every two cups of syrup add ¼ cup of sugar, heat it to boiling, and pour it back over the fruit. Do the same thing the next day and so on until the syrup becomes really thick. After a week remove and drain the fruit on a cake rack and leave it for a week to dry. Pack it in cardboard boxes.

Bottling fruit

You will need vacuum sealing bottles, preferably a bottling thermometer and a pan deep enough to allow the jars to be completely covered with water. The jars must not touch the sides or the bottom of the pan so stand them on a grill grid, cake stand, or make a wooden criss-cross stand. Wash and scald the jars or bottles, the lids and rubber seals in boiling water before using them. Wash the fruit and put it into the bottles mixed with a syrup of 8 oz. of sugar to one pint of water (or use honey or golden syrup) boiled for two minutes and then allowed to cool. Pour it into the jars to the brim and remove air bubbles with a plastic spatula round the sides of the jar.

Put the caps on, but not too tightly (to allow for expansion), put the bottles in the pan and cover them with water. Put on the lid and bring the water slowly to 165° F and keep it there for ten minutes. Remove the bottles with a cloth and immediately tighten the caps — to test, after the bottles have cooled, unscrew the metal caps and lift the bottles by the glass discs; if there is a proper seal they will hold because of the vacuum inside. Label and store in a cool, dark place.

Apricots, cherries, currants, damsons, citrus fruits, peaches, gooseberries and plums need a temperature of 180° F for 15 minutes. Tomatoes can be bottled in the same way but fill the bottles with brine and keep at 190° F for ½ hour. To bottle vegetables you must use a pressure cooker (see your pressure cooker book).

If you want to make your own baby food the fruit should be boiled soft enough to be forced through a sieve, or put in a blender.

Pickles

To pickle means to preserve fruit or vegetables in salt and vinegar. Pickles are best made from firm specimens like green tomatoes, onions, garlic, peas, carrots, cauliflower, beets, red cabbage, radishes and cucumbers. The vinegar for pickling should be prepared beforehand by mixing it with herbs and spices in a basin, standing the basin in a pan of boiling water for a short while and leave to cool. Strain off the herbs and spices. Cut up whatever you want to pickle and sprinkle it well with salt and let it stand for a day. Leave onions to soak in brine. Rinse the salt off and put it into a jar covered with the vinegar. If you like your pickles crisp (red cabbage, for example) use cold vinegar, and boiling vinegar for softer versions, like beetroot.

Chutneys

Can be made from almost anything you are likely to grow, although apple, tomato and marrow are the favourites. Chop the vegetables or fruits up very finely and simmer them with onions, spices and sugar in some vinegar. When it has reduced to a thick slodge pour it into bottles, cover the tops with greaseproof paper and put the lids on.

TOMATO CHUTNEY (the ingredients work well for other chutneys too)

1 lb. green tomatoes, cut up
½ lb. chopped onions
1 oz. salt
2 tsp. cayenne pepper
1¼ pints vinegar
¼ lb. brown sugar or honey
½ lb. raisins
1 oz. whole allspice

After cutting up the vegetables into small pieces, sprinkle them with salt and leave them overnight. Rinse and drain. Boil vinegar with spices for a few minutes then strain off allspice. Then boil everything up together.

PICCALILLI

2 cauliflowers
2 cucumbers
2 lb. shallots or small onions
1 small marrow
1 oz. whole allspice
1 quart vinegar
3 tsp. plain flour
4 oz. sugar
2 tsp. ground ginger
3 tsp. mustard
1½ tsp. turmeric powder

Make in the same way as tomato chutney.

Sauces and Juices

APPLE SAUCE:

Peel, slice and core apples and simmer in a little water. Pass through a sieve and add sugar. Reheat till boiling and then pour into jars. Other sauces are made in a similar way — basically they are no more than sieved chutneys.

TOMATO JUICE:

Simmer tomatoes and pass through a sieve. Add some water, sugar, salt and pepper and bring to boil. Pour into hot bottles, stand for ten minutes in boiling water and seal.

BERRY JUICE:

Simmer and crush berries and strain through a sieve or cheesecloth. Add sugar or honey, a little water and boil. Pour into hot jars and process at 190° F in a hot pan of water (see bottling).

Salting

One final method of preserving, and one of the oldest, that you might like to try is salting runner beans, carrots, beets or turnips. And even corn, if you first remove it from the cob. Use a non-metal container (a glass or stone jar) and store the vegetables in alternate layers of household salt, roughly 1 lb. of household salt to every 3 lb. of corn. Pack them down tightly to exclude the air and weight the top layer down with a plate. Cover with cheesecloth. After a week or so the salt will have drawn all the liquid out of the vegetables so that they will stand in a brine made from their own juices. Add more layers, always topping off with salt, as they shrink, and cover the jar with plastic seal.

Pints		Litres	Gallons		Litres
1.760	1	0.568	0.220	1	4.546
3.520	2	1.137	0.440	2	9.092
5.279	3	1.705	0.660	3	13.638
7.039	4	2.273	0.880	4	18.184
8.799	5	2.841	1.100	5	22.731
10.559	6	3.410	1.320	6	27.277
12.318	7	3.978	1.540	7	31.823
14.078	8	4.546	1.760	8	36.369
15.838	9	5.114	1.980	9	40.915

Ounces		Grams	Pounds		Kilograms
0.035	1	28.350	2.205	1	0.454
0.071	2	56.699	4.409	2	0.907
0.106	3	85.049	6.614	3	1.361
0.141	4	113.398	8.181	4	1.818
0.176	5	141.748	11.023	5	2.268
0.212	6	170.097	13.228	6	2.722
0.247	7	198.447	15.432	7	3.175
0.282	8	226.796	17.637	8	3.629
0.317	9	255.146	19.842	9	4.082

Inches		Milli-metres	Feet		Metres
0.039	1	25.4	3.281	1	0.305
0.079	2	50.8	6.562	2	0.610
0.118	3	76.2	9.843	3	0.914
0.157	4	101.6	13.123	4	1.219
0.197	5	127.0	16.404	5	1.524
0.236	6	152.4	19.685	6	1.829
0.276	7	177.8	22.966	7	2.134
0.315	8	203.2	26.247	8	2.438
0.354	9	228.6	29.528	9	2.743

FURTHER READING

The ABC of preserving (London, H.M.S.O., 1969)

Atkins, F.C., *Mushroom growing today* (Faber, London, 1974)

Baylis, Maggie, *House plants for the purple thumb* (Pitmans, London, 1976).

Bean, Cleeland, 'Bee Keeping', *Ecologist*, October 1974

Bravery, H.E. & Furner, B.G., *Home made wine making and vine growing* (Macdonald, London, 1973)

Brown, E.T., *Garden poultry keeping* (Hutchinson, London, 1930)

————, *Make your garden feed you* (Literary Press, Glasgow, 1940)

Byers, Anthony, *Growing under glass* (Pelham, London, 1974)

Clapham, S., *The Greenhouse book* (David & Charles, London, 1974)

Coulter, Francis C., *A manual of home vegetable gardening* (Dover, N.Y., 1973)

Davis, Adelle, *Let's cook it right* (Allen & Unwin, London, 1963)

Henry Doubleday Research Association, *Pest Control without poisons* (Bocking, Braintree, Essex)

Douglas, J. Sholto, *Beginners guide to hydroponics* (Pelham, London, 1972)

Evans, Hazel, *Good Housekeeping — Small space gardening* (Ebury Press, London, 1974)

Field, Xenia, *Window box gardening* (Pan, London, 1965)

Field, Xenia, *Gardening from scratch* (Hamlyn, London, 1973)

Flawn, Louis N., *Gardening with cloches* (Gifford, London, 1971)

————, *Gardening under glass* (Gifford, London, 1971)

————, *Vegetable gardening for health and flavour* (Bartholomew, London, 1974)

Furner, B.G., *Fresh food from small gardens* (Stuart & Watkins, London, 1969)

————, *Organic vegetable growing* (Macdonald, London, 1973)

————, *The kitchen garden* (Pan, London, 1971)

Gemmell, Alan, *The Sunday gardener* (Elm Tree Books, London, 1973)

Genders, Roy, *The complete book of vegetables and herbs* (Ward Lock, London, 1972)

————, (Ed.), *Pears encyclopedia of gardening* (Pelham, London, 1973)

————, *The epicure's garden* (Pelham, London, 1973)

Grounds, R., *Grow your own vegetables* (Ward Lock, London, 1975)

Harris, Cyril C. & Howells, Marion, *Modern ways of growing and cooking vegetables* (Pelham, London, 1972)

Hemphill, R., *Herbs for all seasons* (Angus & Robertson, Sydney & London, 1972)

Hills, L.D., *Grow your own fruit and vegetables* (Faber, London, 1971)

Hunter, B.T., *The natural foods cookbook* (Faber, London, 1975)

Israel, R. & Slay, R., *Homesteaders' handbook* (Dover, N.Y., 1973)

Kaysing, Bill, *First time farmer's guide* (Straight Arrow, San Francisco, 1973)

Langer, Richard W., *Grow it* (Avon, N.Y., 1972)

Laurel, Alicia Bay, *Living on the earth* (Wildwood House, London, 1973)

Loads, F.W., *Vegetables in the small garden* (Pitman, London, 1949)

Loewenfeld, Claire, *Herb Gardening* (Faber, London, 1970)

Loewenfeld, Claire & Back, Phillipa, *Herbs for health and cookery* (Pan, London, 1965)

Mabey, Richard, *Food for free* (Collins, London, 1972)

Mead, Cicely, *A concise guide to vegetable gardening* (Muller, London, 1971)

Ministry of Agriculture, *Chemicals for gardens* (H.M.S.O., London, 1965)

————, *How to manage an allotment* (H.M.S.O., London, 1917)

Morse, R.A., *The complete guide to beekeeping* (Pelham, London, 1972)

National Federation of Women's Institutes, *Preservation* (London, 1972)

————, *Unusual preserves* (London, 1972)

Pople, David, *Growing vegetables* (Studio Vista, London, 1968)

Portsmouth, John, *Teach yourself modern poultry keeping* (Teach Yourself Books, London, 1973)

(ed.) Rodale, Robert & Furner, Brian, *The basic book of organic gardening* (Pan/Ballantine, London, New York, 1972)

Sandford, J.C., *The domestic rabbit* (C. Lockwood, London, 1962)

Seymour, John & Sally, *Self Sufficiency* (Faber, London, 1974)

Shewell-Cooper, W.E., *The complete vegetable grower* (Faber, London, 1955)

Simons, Arthur J., *The new vegetable grower's handbook* (Penguin, Harmondsworth, 1975)

Stevenson, Violet, *Patio, rooftop and balcony gardening* (Collingridge, London, 1967)

Sudell, Richard, *Practical gardening in pictures* (Oldhams, London, 1967)

(ed.) Sunset books, *Vegetable gardening* (Lane books, California, 1974)

Survival Scrapbook 2 Food (Unicorn books, Brighton/Seattle, 1972)

(ed.) Thompson, Alan, *Your smallholding* (Penguin, London, 1947)

Thomas, Anna, *Vegetarian epicure* (Penguin, Harmondsworth, 1973)

Thrower, Percy, *Fresh vegetables and herbs from your garden* (Hamlyn, London, 1974)

The vegetable garden displayed (Royal Horticultural Society, London, 1974)

Wickers, David & Tuey, John, *How to make things grow* (for children) (Studio Vista, London, 1972)

(ed.) Wright, Michael, *The complete indoor gardener* (Pan, London, 1973)

Suppliers of hydroponic nutrients:

Hydroponic Chemical Co Inc., Box 97C, Copley, Ohio

Chas. C. Gilbert & Co., Ivy St., San Diego 1, California

Suttons of Reading Ltd., Reading, Berkshire

Luwasa (Horticulture) Ltd., 189 Bedfont Lane, Feltham, Middlesex

Bowden Hydroponics, Maynard O'Connor (Pty) Ltd., Bowden, Adelaide, S. Australia

INDEX

Acidity, soil 11
Alfalfa 57
Alkalinity, soil 11
Allotments 46
Apples 142, 143
Apple sauce 167
Artificial lighting 54, 55
Artichokes, globe 79
Artichokes, Jerusalem 80
Asparagus 81
Aubergine (egg plant) 65, 83
Automatic watering methods 73, 74

Balconies 49—51
Basil 70
Bay tree 66
Beans 75, 85
Beans, broad 85, 86
Beans, dwarf French 86
Beans, runner 88
Beetroot 89, 90
Berries 152, 153
Berry juice 167
Blackberries 152,
Blackcurrants 153—5
Borscht 91
Bottling fruit 164, 165
Bouquet garni 67
Brassicas 28, 29
Broccoli 91, 92
Broths 158
Brussels sprouts 92—4
Brussels sprouts slaw 94

Cabbages 91—6
Calabrese 91
Candied fruit 163
Capsicums 125, 126
Carrot plant 75
Carrots 96, 97
Catch cropping 18
Cauliflower 99
Cauliflower curry 99, 100
Celery 101, 102
Celeriac 101, 102
Chard, Swiss 105
Chervil 70
Chicory 105, 106
Children and growing things 75
Chives 70
Chutney 165, 166
Climbers 63
Cloche 37, 38
Cold frame 36, 37
Compost 11—14
Containers 60—62
Cooking vegetables 156—9
Cordons, fruit 153

Courgettes 116—18
Cucumbers 107, 108
Currants 153—5

Devilled tomatoes 140
Dibber 8
Dig For Victory campaign 1
Digging 9—11
Dill 66
Diseases 41—3
Draw hoe 7
Drying 160—62
Dutch hoe 7
Dwarf French beans 86

Egg plant 83
Endive 115, 116

F.1. Hybrids 24
Fennel (or Finnochio) 109
Fennel à la niçoise 109
Fertilizers 14, 72
Figs 146
Fines herbes 67
First Fistuqia 86
Fork 7
Freezing 159, 160
Fruit 152—6
Fruit pudding 155, 156
Fruit soufflé 155

Garden lime 7
Garlic 70
Germination 31
Globe artichokes 79
Gooseberries 153
Grapes 146, 147
Greenhouse 36

Half hardy varieties 25
Hand trowel and fork 7, 8
Hardening off 32
Hardy varieties 25
Haricot soup 87
Herb bread 67
Herb tea 67
Herbs 62, 65—70
Hoeing 39, 40
Holiday care 73
Hose 7
Humus 12
Hydroponics 57—60

Iced cucumber soup 109
Indoor farming 51—3
Intercropping 19
Jams 162
Jerusalem artichokes 80

Kale 111
Kohl-rabi 112, 113
Korean spinach 133

Leeks 113, 114
Lettuces 115, 116
Lime 11
Loam 9

Marjoram 70
Manure 12
Marrows 63, 116—18
Measuring rod 7
Melons 63, 147, 148
Minestrone 118
Mint 70
Moisture meter 72
Muesli 155
Mulching 40
Mung beans 56
Mushrooms 55, 62
Mustard and cress 56

Nets 8
Nitrogen 12

Office farming 54
Onions 119, 120
Onion soup 120, 121
Organic waste 12
Other people's gardens 46, 47
Overwintering 19

Parsley 70
Parsnip croquettes 122
Parsnips 122
Patios 50
Peanuts 76
Peas 124, 125
Peat 9
Peat pellets 30
Peat pots 30
Pelleted seeds 23
Permanent crops 15
Peppers 65, 125, 126
Pests 41—3
Phosphorous 12
Piccalilli 166
Pickles 165
Pip plants 75
Pollination 73
Potash 12
Potato and leek pie 114
Potato plant 75
Potatoes 127—9
Potting compost 32
Pricking out 31, 32
Propagation 29—31
Pruning 145

Pumpkin 76, 77
Pumpkin pie 77

Radishes 129, 130
Raised beds 51
Raspberry canes 152
Ratatouille 157, 158
Redcurrants 153—5
Repotting 35
Rhubarb 148, 149
Roof farming 50, 51
Rosemary 70
Rotation 15—17
Runner beans 88

Sage 70
Salads 63
Salsify 131
Salting 167
Sauces and juices 167
Saving seeds 24
Scorzonera 131
Seed beds 28, 29
Seed compost 30, 31
Seeds 23—32
Shallots 119, 120
Soil testing 11

Soil types 9
Sowing seeds and climate 25
Sowing seeds indoors 29—32
Sowing seeds outdoors 26—8
Soups 158
Space 3
Spade 7
Spinach 133
Spit 18
Sprouting vegetables 56, 57, 63
Storing fruit and vegetables 159—67
Strawberries 63, 150, 151
Stuffed marrow 118
Stuffed peppers 127
Succession cropping 18
Successional sowing 19
Suffolk carrot pie 97
Summer savoury 70
Summer squash 116—18
Sunflowers 76
Swedes 134
Sweet and sour cabbage 96
Sweet corn 134—7
Swiss chard 105

Tarragon 70
Tarragon vinegar 67
Tender varieties 25

Terraces 50
Thinning seedlings 28
Thyme 70
Tilth 26
Tomato chutney 166
Tomato juice 167
Tomatoes 64, 137—40
Tools 6—8
Transplanting 32—5
Turnips 141, 142

Vegetable casserole 157
Vegetable soufflé 159
Vegetable spaghetti 118
Verandahs 50
Vinaigrette sauce 158

Water spray 8
Watering 38, 72, 73
Watering can 7, 8
Weeds and weeding 8, 39, 40
White currants 153
Window boxes 47

Yoghurt 71
Zuccini 116—18

Food for Free

RICHARD MABEY

Food for Free is an illustrated guide to the astonishing — and often delectable — range of wild British foods. Richard Mabey describes over 300 foods, including shellfish, fungi and seaweed, as well as edible roots and weeds, flowers and fruit. He discusses the nutritional and gastronomical value of each plant and gives guidance on how to find, gather and cook it.

Food for Free is a rich storehouse of anecdote, information and recipe, promising entertainment in the kitchen and ceaseless diversion on country walks.

'A superb and carefully compiled guide . . . the theme is that this island has an abundant store of free, wild food.' *Grimsby Evening Telegraph*

'Marjorie Blamey's illustrations are as delectable as the text. All in all, a book properly described as delicious.' *Sunday Times*

Large format. Fully illustrated.

Country Bazaar

ANDY PITTAWAY and BERNARD SCOFIELD

A handbook to country pleasures

Churning butter, tracking badgers,
Making rugs from home-dyed wool;
Finding clay and master-thatchers,
A spinning wheel or milking stool.

Throwing pots and pressing flowers,
Collecting honey and teasing yarn;
Making sun-dials tell the hours,
Keeping chickens in the barn.

Knots and sheep and goats and rambles,
Brasses, bees and animal spoor;
Baskets, trees and wayside brambles,
Smocks and shells and lots, lots more.

'This loving patchwork of crafts, folklore . . . has something for
everybody.' *The Vegetarian*

'. . . a true rustic revel — innocent, sensual, joyous, gloriously
chaotic, but with its feet always firmly on the earth.' Richard
Mabey

'Glorious book of country pursuits, beautifully illustrated.'
Time Out

Special large format. Lavishly illustrated throughout.

Not Just A Load of Old Lentils

ROSE ELLIOT

For the converted and the carniverous alike — a gourmet's guide to the best of vegetarian cookery.

Widely praised as one of the very best of vegetarian cookery books, Rose Elliot's 400 varied recipes will stimulate the converted to be more adventurous, and provide bored meat-eaters with a unique source of appetizing ideas — *Savoury Pie, Chinese Fried Rice, Courgette au Gratin, Mushroom Soufflé* and many more.

Combining a practical approach to the preparation of healthy meals with a dash of *haute cuisine*, these recipes banish once and for all the ogre of hard nut-cutlets and limp lettuce leaves.

' . . . a "must" on the kitchen shelf of those, not only vegetarians, who pride themselves on providing their families with meals of interest and variety.' *Span*

' . . . interesting and stimulating . . . recipes which cry out to be tried.' *Health for All*

' . . . a joy to use . . . ' *The Vegetarian*

The Sunday Gardener

Edited by ALAN GEMMELL

How, in a busy weekend, to cope with: the lawn; the fruit trees; the flowers; the greenhouse; the shrubs; the vegetable patch; pests, diseases, weeds and the house plants.

*Two exciting cookery books from Ursel
and Derek Norman . . .*

Use Your Loaf

Use Your Loaf . . . and bake your *own* bread: the Old English
Farmhouse Loaf, the French Loaf, Grandmama's Milk Bread,
Monastery Oatmeal Bread, Pumpernickel — Chicago Style,
Country Oatmeal Rye, Croissants, Viennese Gugelhupf, Bara
Brith and many more.

Use Your Loaf . . . there's no mystique about it. Ursel Norman's
step-by-step recipes and Derek Norman's delightful pictures
make it simple and fun to do.

Salad Days

Salad Days are full and warm, the food crisp, colourful and
succulent. Green salads make a start, but more exotic feasts
from France or Germany, Spain or Greece, Russia or Mexico,
are as easy to put together and yet more delicious to eat.

Ursel and Derek Norman show how, on their own or served with
fish or meat, familiar ingredients like beetroot, peppers, cabbage,
mushrooms, onions, chicory, fruit and nuts, can readily combine
to produce salads that add interest to any day of the year.

Large format. Fully illustrated.

A FONTANA SELECTION

Keep Smiling Through

SUSAN BRIGGS

All the nostalgia of everyday life in war-time Britain, superbly captured in a fascinating book introduced by Vera Lynn. Lavishly illustrated throughout with full-colour and black-and-white pictures from a host of contemporary sources.

Scotch Whisky

DAVID DAICHES

A colourful, affectionate and complete history of Scotch whisky from its early days as a cottage industry to the triumph of the great blending firms and the decline in popularity of the single malts in the present century. In his final chapters, he takes a connoisseur's look at the different qualities of individual malt whiskies; discriminating and knowledgeable, his one criterion is enjoyment.

Eat Fat and Grow Slim

RICHARD MACKARNESS

Richard Mackarness, a doctor and psychiatrist, presents a revolutionary and fully tested approach to slimming that encourages you to eat as much good food as you want while ignoring the calorie problem completely. How it works is clearly explained in the new and fully revised edition of this best-selling work, an immensely successful medically approved guide to the relationship between food and health.